Everything That Makes Me Happy I Learned when I Grew Up

RAY S. ANDERSON

InterVarsity Press
Downers Grove, Illinois

InterVarsity Press® is the book-publishing division of InterVarsity Christian Fellowship®, a student movement active on campus at hundreds of universities, colleges and schools of nursing in the United States of America, and a member movement of the International Fellowship of Evangelical Students. For information about local and regional activities, write Public Relations Dept., InterVarsity Christian Fellowship, 6400 Schroeder Rd., P.O. Box 7895, Madison, WI 53707-7895.

Scripture quotations, unless otherwise noted, are from the New Revised Standard Version of the Bible, copyright 1989 by the Division of Christian Education of the National Council of the Churches of Christ in the U.S.A., and are used by permission.

"Do Not Go Gentle into That Good Night," from Dylan Thomas: Poems of Dylan Thomas. Copyright 1952 by Dylan Thomas. Reprinted by pemission of New Directions Pub. Corp.

"Even" from THE UNICORN AND OTHER POEMS by Anne Morrow Lindbergh. Copyright © 1956 by Anne Morrow Lindbergh. Reprinted by permission of Pantheon Books, a division of Random House, Inc.

"The Friend" excerpted with permission of Simon & Schuster, Inc. from Letters and Papers from Prison, revised, enlarged edn. by Dietrich Bonhoeffer. Copyright © 1953, 1967, 1971 by SCM Press Ltd and the Macmillan Co.

Excerpt from "The Hollow Men" in COLLECTED POEMS 1909-1962 by T. S. Eliot, copyright 1936 by Faber and Faber Ltd and Harcourt Brace & Company, copyright © 1964, 1963 by T. S. Eliot, reprinted by permission of the publishers.

ISBN 0-8308-1642-9

Printed in the United States of America

Library of Congress Cataloging-in-Publication Data
Anderson, Ray Sherman.
    Everything that makes me happy I learned when I grew up/Ray S.
Anderson.
      p.   cm.
    Includes bibliographical references.
    ISBN 0-8308-1642-9
    1. Emotional maturity—Religious aspects—Christianity.
  2. Christian life.   I. Title.
  BV4509.5.A56   1995
  248.8'4—dc20   95-7842
                                                                CIP

19 18 17 16 15 14 13 12 11 10 9 8 7 6 5 4 3 2 1
10 09 08 07 06 05 04 03 02 01 00 99 98 97 96 95

For Myla,
a loving sister
and a loyal friend

What Is
Happiness?

Were you unhappy as a child?"
The question followed my announcement of a possible subtitle to a
book: *Everything That Makes Me Unhappy I Learned as a Child.*

"Not at all," I responded. "I'm not writing about an unhappy
childhood but about why adults are often so unhappy without really
knowing why."

"So, then, you are an unhappy adult?"

"Certainly not!" I replied, a little too emphatically. I had to admit,
however, that I was not happy with the direction that this conversation
had taken.

To be sure, we are all unhappy at times about something that
happens to us that makes our day and life uncomfortable, if not
outright painful. I am no Pollyanna who insists that there is a silver

lining in every storm cloud. Considerable wind and rain accompany some of those clouds. Everyone has negative experiences, even happy people. But the truly happy are those who have the strength to bear weakness, who have the courage to face their fears and whose embrace of life enlarges through every loss.

Happiness is not the gentle stroke of good luck, nor is it the sensuous power of success. Good luck sets us up for the sucker punch of a blow to the solar plexus at the moment we have raised our hands above our heads in praise to the gods of fortune and fame. Success is a miserable companion on the way to the top and a fair-weather friend on the way down.

The instant euphoria of winning the lottery, sacking the quarterback or finding your size and color on the bargain table is a perishable product. Happiness is neither absence of pain nor freedom from care and anxiety. Happiness is indefinable except by those who possess it. Happiness is acquired; it is not a birthright.

The belief that happiness is a natural gift possessed by the child and stolen by the misfortunes of life is a myth created by unhappy adults who long for the "age of innocence." Unhappiness is a mythology, with a devil to be blamed for sowing the seeds of failure and frustration in the soil from which we were formed. Unhappiness seems to be the consequence of losing our childhood and the price we pay for establishing a beachhead on the mainland of maturity. In this mythology of childhood happiness, we cherish our nostalgia and cling with painful memory to the losses we cannot give up.

In the biblical story we endow Adam and Eve with an innocent happiness before the Fall. They are children, we suppose, whose innocence was joy and whose happiness was perfect. But this is to read the story through our own myth. The Bible tells us that the original creation was "good," not "happy." They were children of promise, whose happiness was found in claiming the promise and living by it, even—or perhaps especially—when it reappeared in the dark night of their failure like a silver moon of hope. They were children of destiny, whose happiness was found in their future, not their past. Happiness is a promise to be realized, not a present to be unwrapped.

How do we acquire true happiness, then, if it belongs to maturity and not to childhood? How were the seeds of unhappiness sown in our childhood years? In part one of this book we demythologize our concept of childhood happiness and see that unhappiness is not the result of suffering the "slings and arrows of outrageous fortune" but, rather, is the result of becoming stuck in our childish ways of responding to life. The theme for this section is set by St. Paul, who in his classic hymn of love wrote, "When I was a child, I spoke like a child, I thought like a child, I reasoned like a child; when I became an adult, I put an end to childish ways" (1 Corinthians 13:11).

In part two we take positive steps toward happiness. I believe that happiness *can* be learned, and I believe that the so-called secret can be understood and practiced. In each of us is the potential for the happy child whom we think we have left behind. To each of us belongs the positive happiness that we mistakenly think has been stolen from us. We turn again to the letters of St. Paul to the early churches: "I have learned to be content with whatever I have. I know what it is to have little, and I know what is to have plenty. In any and all circumstances I have learned the secret of being well-fed and of going hungry, of having plenty and of being in need" (Philippians 4:11-12).

In part three we explore the dynamics of happiness in the context of the shared promises of life. Examining various relationships, we find healing for unhappiness and hope for those who are seeking happiness.

Did I have an unhappy childhood? Not at all. It was a "good" childhood, and it prepared me for the happiness that I now cherish. More and more the happy child within me grows as I grow into life, and toward the promise of life that flows eternally from the heart of God.

I wish to express appreciation to my editor, Rodney Clapp, and especially to my two copy editors, Betsy Rossen Elliot and Ruth Goring, for their insightful and creative help in preparing the final manuscript. They felt the pulse of my own heart and made the process a happy one!

Part 1

Everything That Makes Me Unhappy I Learned as a Child

1

Someone Else
Always Has
More Toys:
Life Is Not Fair

*A*t the age of twenty months, my grandson Brandon had what I considered to be his fair share of toys. As he played outside with the neighbor children, a fair ecological balance seemed to be in effect. But happiness is a fragile experience in the toyland of childhood.

The yellow car Thomas was sitting in captured Brandon's imagination. Walking right up to it, he tried to push Thomas out and crawl in himself. The consternation in Thomas's face was exceeded only by the bright-eyed zeal in the eyes of Brandon, who—despite being outpointed in age and size—sought to take physical ownership of what had already become his by desire.

The result? Two unhappy little boys. One denied access to a toy he truly needed to be happy, the other desperately gripping the steering wheel of a car with fear and trembling.

For Thomas the fun had gone out of the toy. It was now a possession to be defended against the unprovoked terrorism of his little friend. Would he ever again be able to play happily with his little yellow car without fear that he might lose it in a moment to his closest playmate? And how about Brandon? Will his stable of toys be sufficient now that he has been denied the one thing on which his heart was set?

The fact that a few hours later the two boys were playing happily together (the yellow car had been confiscated by parental discretion) reminds us how quickly happiness can be restored when the attention span is short. Yet a lesson has been learned, the first lesson of childhood unhappiness: Someone else always has more toys. Life is not fair. What your heart desires your hands cannot acquire. What is rightfully yours can be lost to another.

"Mine, Mine, Mine!"

Psychologists tell us that the primal motivation of the infant is for gratification of the pleasure need. In technical terms, this is called narcissism. It is not merely a fascination with one's own bodily feelings but a deep-seated pleasure instinct that caregivers cater to so as to arouse response from the infant. This "infantile narcissism," some claim, is the core of the self and the source of most responses that are essential to the development of the child.

Attached to this pleasure need is a "primitive moral instinct," which is also reinforced by parents and other caregivers. When a child tears off the wrapping paper on a birthday present, the child is expected to receive the toy with unrestrained pleasure and joy. When he or she doesn't respond this way, the parents receive a devastating blow to their own narcissistic needs. They desire that their gratification in giving will exceed their guilt for spending too much. If the child has siblings, great efforts are made to reinforce the sense of ownership of this new toy. "This is yours, Brandon, all yours to enjoy and play with. It's your birthday—a special day for a special little boy!"

Certain lessons have been subtly communicated to the child through this ritual of gift giving. First, others are present to fulfill his pleasure and to make him happy. His pleasure is desired and rewarded when he expresses it. "There you go. Doesn't Mom always know just what toy you'll like?" Second, a sense of ownership goes with what gives pleasure. The toys are not only to give pleasure but also to give rights and privileges. "Here, Brandon, we'll put your name on this so you'll always know it's yours."

Through these rituals the inner life of the child is being formed. The child gradually develops a sense of belonging, self-worth and identity. One "belongs" to those who are the source of well-being, who provide comfort, give pleasure and reward response.

The child's world is extended through attachment to those primary caregivers and, later, to the secondary caregivers—the familiar baby sitter and the mysterious grandparents who come and go without warning. The child's self is extended through attachment to the objects that give security (the blanket), gratification (the pacifier) and pleasure (toys). This identity is shaped through what some psychologists call "ego formation." The ego is the sense of self that the child develops. It can be considered the basis for the "primitive moral instincts" that give the child a feeling of outrage when he or she is denied access to gratification and pleasure.

When Thomas reacted instinctively to protect his yellow car, his small world was threatened. The threat wasn't just denial of the pleasure that he himself received by playing with the car. He felt a deeper threat to his own identity, as though his basic rights were being violated. And they were! He had been led to feel that this was "his car," that he alone had the right to play with it. Without knowing it, he reacted morally and justly against the violation of his rights, even though he lacked the moral wisdom to respond appropriately.

Brandon, on the other hand, also felt a moral right to fulfill his own pleasure need by taking possession of the car. For while he had learned well the lesson of what belongs to him, he had no sense of what belongs to Thomas. For Brandon, pleasure and ownership blended into a single passion. When deprived of what gave him pleasure, he had the same moral instincts as when he was deprived of that which belongs to him. He reacted with the "moral outrage" felt when desire is frustrated.

A Certain Logic to It

This scenario explodes the myth of the happy child and reveals to us the logic of unhappiness. Being deprived of that which gives pleasure does not alone create unhappiness. That need can be quenched with a new dose of pleasure or a new toy. Unhappiness is the deeply felt unfairness of life when our toys are taken away or when the toy we need to give us pleasure is possessed by someone else.

Once we have experienced as children the powerful feeling of unfairness when denied gratification, either of ownership or of desires, happiness becomes the sugar coating on the bitter pill of life's injustice. The pleasure has no sooner dissolved in our mouth than the sour taste of grief over unfulfilled desire spreads over our tongue. The bitter bile of anger over life's unfairness rises up in our throat, more powerful than the sweetest honey.

This does not happen all at once, of course. Nor do all children grow up to be unhappy adults. We are talking here not about unhappy children but about the chronic unhappiness many adults live with. We are probing the unhappiness that pervades the lives of so many to discover its inner logic. If chronic adult unhappiness really is rooted in a sense of unfairness, this may well have been learned as a child and carried over into the adult. The fusion of the pleasure instinct with power of ownership produces the "childish" behavior to which the apostle Paul referred when he wrote, "When I was a child, I spoke like a child, I thought like a child, I reasoned like a child; when I became an adult, I put an end to childish ways" (1 Corinthians 13:11).

When Al and Lydia came to me for counseling, their marriage was almost shattered by conflicts over family finances. Both were professionals; their combined salaries provided the family with what appeared to be more than adequate income. Yet they were deeply in debt, with credit card charges up to the limit. "We went to a financial consultant," Lydia said, "but we even got into a fight about taking the recommended steps to get our budget back on a realistic basis."

Al added, "We fight over money, but I don't think that is the problem. We are probably the most unhappy people I know. I think we would each be happier if we separated and went our own ways."

"What was it like when you were single and living alone?" I asked. "Were you happier then?"

The responses were revealing. "I really didn't think about being happy," Lydia answered slowly. "I had enough money to buy nice clothes, and my folks gave me the sports car I had always wanted when I graduated from college. Still, I longed for the happiness that would be mine when I found the right man and had a beautiful wedding. I think I was happy when we were first married, but we began to argue about everything, and that was the end of that. I dreamed that marriage would be heaven on earth, but in reality it has been a hellish nightmare."

"I've been on my own since graduating from high school," Al replied. "My parents were divorced and I lived with my mother. I bought my own car with money I earned while still in school working part time. I worked to pay my way through college and landed a job with a top law firm.

"When I met Lydia I thought I'd found a perfect partner. She had a kind of independence that I appreciated and a carefree spirit that made her fun to be with. We were really happy before we were married. But once we started to live together, I felt like I had lost control of my life. She became very possessive of me, and I guess that I have really resented that. Anyway, being married is not much fun."

Al and Lydia are both adults. Both have grown up and left childhood behind them. Or have they?

The unhappiness both of them feel is a pervasive and destructive aspect of their marriage. Each believes that the only solution is to end the marriage and start over, hoping to find the illusive happiness that they feel is denied them by the marriage partner. They are puzzled by their own emotions and reactions. They feel caught up in a tangle of threads that are hopelessly knotted in the wrong places. They went to a dance and ended in a brawl.

A Not-So-Tender Trap

When we get stuck in unhappiness, we no longer remember how to be happy. Our instincts tell us to shake off the unhappiness and dump what malfunctions, like getting rid of a car that has plagued us with constant breakdowns. If we can't win, we can at least cut our losses. There are no happy divorces, no pleasant partings when the playground becomes the battlefield. Because we are adults now, we think unhappiness should be handled in an adult way, yet we inevitably seek happiness as an antidote to a lost childhood.

Happiness is the rush of fresh air that pours through the opening we have torn through the suffocating envelope of despair. Happiness is the relief when the pill dulls the pain; it is the instant stimulation of a chemical substance. Happiness is the emotional high of starting a new relationship, acquiring a new toy, betting on the Super Bowl winner.

When happiness is sought as the solution for unhappiness, it is fated from the beginning not to survive the next crisis. Consequently, when the happiness that we seek as the cure for unhappiness unravels, we either turn to another source for happiness or begin to deal with our unhappiness. Often it helps to seek help from trained counselors. We need insight as to which knot to cut, courage to smash some idol, a space to vent our rage and to grieve our losses.

Why have Al and Lydia come for help? They don't really know, except that their unhappiness has no end. We talk. I ask them to tell me how it feels to have been denied the happiness they expected in life. They have difficulty expressing these feelings. Emotions have become like frozen ropes holding two ships together in a frigid and stormy sea.

It finally hurts too much to hold back. The tears come, even sobs. "Why would God allow this to happen? Its so unfair. I desired nothing but what God wanted me to have, and I believed Al was God's gift to me for a husband. If we can't trust God to give us what is good, what can we trust? I feel betrayed, even punished."

Al is shocked and stricken by what Lydia has said. "I don't know who you thought I was, but I was not a prize to be awarded to you by God like your father giving you a sports car. I never had anything but what I earned for myself, and you took that from me. I thought we agreed to share our lives, not to live each other's life. You weren't happy until you got control of my private life, and now that doesn't seem to have made you happy either!"

I think back to Brandon and Thomas and the bright yellow car. I think of the lessons that each learned, how unfair it is when the thing you cherish the most is denied to you. In their childish outrage I see the beginning of a future unhappiness, waiting to be triggered by some intrusion into the space created by desires and dignity.

Al and Lydia have in common this unresolved moral outrage at the unfairness of life when each has experienced a loss. For Al, the "yellow car" is his by right of ownership. He has internalized it as a possession that is as dear as his most intimate self and as precious as the boundary by which he defines himself over and against the unfriendly world. When that boundary is violated, he is offended and outraged.

Lydia, on the other hand, has a claim to the "yellow car" by virtue of both desire and promise. From her parents she learned that what her heart was set on was hers to expect and to claim as gift. When that expectation is violated, when she doesn't get what she had hoped for, she feels betrayed and angry.

When Al and Lydia met, they began as playmates, with a playground big enough to permit both her desire and his dignity. She didn't demand the "yellow car" immediately, for her claim was on it in the future. He did not sense a threat, for his sense of independence and dignity of self were a guarantee to her of what lay ahead. But they were already on a collision course, and the "yellow car" that they both possessed and desired would become a source of frustration and grief.

A Moral Dilemma

The inner logic of unhappiness is the fusion of the pleasure instinct with a sense of ownership of all that lies within one's grasp. Children quickly assume that things given to them to enjoy belong to them. Their basic instinct is to tie self-gratification to ownership of that which provides it. Just try to get back a set of car keys you had given to a child to play with!

When the pleasure instinct is frustrated, a primitive moral instinct arises that leads to outrage. When the car keys are finally taken away, we are left with an unhappy child. The source of much adult unhappiness is thus learned as a child and reinforced through the experiences of childhood and young adulthood.

Inevitably each infant will experience this kind of unhappiness to some degree, for the self is incapable in its earliest stages of development to accept the moral value of delayed gratification. The pleasure instinct and a sense of ownership are fused before there is a chance for the self to differentiate between feelings of pleasure and feelings of power. Having the pleasure instinct gratified gives one an immediate sense of power. The infant experiences a feeling of being all-powerful when he or she receives gratification from those who are ready to give it.

This sense of being all-powerful is an acquired feeling; it is not innate, as is the pleasure instinct. We are not born with a sense of power, but each of us possesses from birth a need for self-fulfillment and instincts for self-gratification. At the core of the pleasure instinct is a deep longing for the fulfillment of self through relation to another. This is one way of understanding the biblical concept of the image of

-created longing seeks fulfillment in its source—that is,

the love of God. Human love and relationship are a reflection of that divine image, which is experienced as a longing and desire for self-fulfillment. There is, in a sense, a "moral right" to this fulfillment, so that if it is denied there is a sense of violation and even injury to the self.

The moral instinct of the self is not found in the sense of ownership so much as in the pleasure instinct. But when the self feels in control and believes that it owns what is needed for self-gratification, the moral instinct shifts from pleasure to power of ownership. The result is that the child confuses pleasure with a sense of ownership and learns to defend what is felt to be rightfully "mine" with great passion.

When the yellow car is confiscated, both Brandon and Thomas are offended, each in his own way. They do not feel a loss of gratification but rather a threat to their very sense of being. No compromise can be accepted, no promise of future pleasure will do. "I want it, and now I can't have it!"

In some cases children can be coaxed out of temper tantrums by an immediate offer of an even greater gratification, such as a double-dip ice-cream cone. But this only compounds the problem. Using pleasure to alleviate a sense of moral outrage is a quick fix of happiness, leaving the underlying unhappiness unhealed and untouched. A deeper longing remains unfulfilled.

Al and Lydia are each caught in the moral dilemma of unhappiness. Each experienced a fusion of pleasure and power of ownership that served well enough when each had a kind of ownership that fulfilled the pleasure instinct. Both were "happy" as long as there was no failure or violation of the boundaries that they had internalized and projected.

Marriage is only one of the arenas of life in which we must learn to find happiness in giving pleasure rather than receiving it. Sooner or later, as each person grows up, he or she is challenged to surrender the right of ownership for the sake of self-fulfillment. At this point, when we allow love to do its work, a new instinct begins to emerge, one that receives gratification from empowering the life of another. Love is acquiring the capacity to experience ultimate meaning and fulfillment of the self in the life of another.

The Key to Happiness

There is a seed from which happiness can grow.

The empowerment of love is one form of the grace of God sent through human parents, the ministry of Christ in Word and Spirit, and the effective intervention of Christian therapists. The longing for self-fulfillment is not the root of sin. Rather, sin emerges through the inherited sense of ownership and autonomy with regard to the Word and law of God. When the pleasure instinct is gratified without observing any boundaries of love, a person feels all-powerful.

The key to happiness is not to annihilate the self but to rediscover the self as an object of God's love. This leads to self-worth and moral worth, with self-fulfillment gained through the intentions and actions of love. When the self is empowered through love, a person can accept delayed gratification. The moral worth of the self is thus affirmed, overcoming the blind moral outrage produced when the instinct for self-gratification is frustrated and a feeling of powerlessness results. The key to happiness is not gratification but self-fulfillment gained through delayed gratification, with self-worth and moral worth affirmed.

So what are Lydia and Al to do? How do we enter back into our childhood to pry apart this fusion between pleasure and the power of ownership? It is never easy and seldom simple.

It begins, as Jesus once said, with becoming "like a child again." "Truly I tell you, whoever does not receive the kingdom of God as a little child will never enter it" (Mark 10:15). When Brandon and Thomas someday seek to enter the kingdom of God, they will have to go back in their hearts and minds to the "yellow car" and relinquish ownership to it.

Happiness is not only the child's delight but also the grownup's feeling of joy and expectation of the future. Happiness is finding the promise of our childhood realized in the productivity of our maturity. True happiness is a state of being, of being blessed by the realization that with God one can suffer loss and still survive. "Blessed [happy] are those who mourn, for they will be comforted," said Jesus in the Sermon on the Mount (Matthew 5:4). This is a kind of happiness that comes as a gift when life is open to God's blessing in and through all circumstances. Happiness is having a sense of well-being, even if one is not feeling well.

When Jesus exhorted us to "receive the kingdom of God as a little child," he meant that we rediscover the longing that opens us up to God's love and the fulfillment of the self in another. It may well be that Jesus was reminding adults that they carry within them a childlike longing, which has become a childish bent toward controlling their own destinies and securing their own gratification through controlling others.

The love of Jesus is an empowering love, aimed at evoking in each of us the desire for the kingdom of God and everything else added to it (Matthew 6:33). God's desire is to give us all things that pertain to life and godliness. Even as adults we may continue to have a childish grasp on the "yellow car," which promises such gratification but leads to such grief and unhappiness. When the longing for self-fulfillment is met through the love of God, we can be empowered to relinquish our toys and reach out for the joy of a shared life.

Al and Lydia can each identify their own "yellow car." And when they do, they will discover that love is more than fair. It is the power to give and to gain in return. The God-created longing hidden in our unhappiness holds the seed of true fulfillment and happiness.

2

Someone Else Always Sets the Rules: *Life Is Not Free*

I was a farm boy, but I attended the primary school in a nearby town. In the spring, when the snow had melted and the ground had warmed, the favorite game at recess and after school was marbles.

Each boy had a small sack of colorful marbles, one of which was the "shooter." Two boys would place some marbles in a circle drawn in the dirt; then, taking turns, each would attempt to shoot the other boy's marbles out of the circle by cradling the shooter in one finger and expelling it with the force of the thumb. If successful, he gained the other's marbles one by one as they were "shot out."

I practiced at home in our farmyard before attempting to play with the "town boys." When I felt proficient, I ventured to play a game with one of the other boys after school. When my turn came I expertly shot a marble out of the circle and claimed it as my own. "That's no good," shouted my opponent. "You have to have your fist touching the ground when you shoot. You didn't and your shot doesn't count!" He took the marble I had claimed and put it back in the circle.

"I never heard of that rule," I protested.

"Well," he answered, "you're playing in town now, and you have to play by our rules."

I promptly picked up my marbles and went home, chagrined and angry. That's one of my earliest recollections of being beaten by rules that someone else set. I must confess, however, that I have "picked up my marbles and gone home" on other occasions as an adult, when someone else's rules spoiled the game for me.

Learning the Rules of Life

Every child soon learns that you can't play a game without rules and that someone else always sets the rules. This is a source of much unhappiness. Games are different from toys. Toys give pleasure because they stimulate the imagination and reward the possessor with self-satisfaction. Toys also tend to create a sense of ownership and power, as we saw in the previous chapter. Games are different in that they ordinarily involve other players and each player must abide by the same rules. My first game of marbles with a town boy collapsed at the outset because we were not playing by the same rules.

When Jesus became frustrated with his contemporaries because they would not receive his teaching concerning the kingdom of God, he once said, "But to what will I compare this generation? It is like children sitting in the marketplaces and calling to one another, 'We played the flute for you, and you did not dance; we wailed, and you did not mourn' " (Matthew 11:16-17).

Scholars tell us that this is a reference to a children's game called "Weddings and Funerals." Some of the children would pretend to be playing at a wedding; the others were supposed to dance. When the first group suddenly pretended to be wailing at a funeral, the others were supposed to stop dancing and join the wailing. In the instance Jesus described, the children were refusing to play the game "by the rules."

Not all rules have to do with games, though. I often wonder how the young boy Jesus felt when his mother rebuked him for wandering away from the family as they began their long journey back to Galilee from Jerusalem. This is the only incident the Bible records of Jesus' childhood (he was twelve years old), and it shows him being scolded for not abiding by family rules. When his parents found him after three days, he was sitting among the teachers in the temple, demonstrating his superior wisdom concerning the law. His mother was apparently not very impressed: "Child, why have you treated us like this? Look, your father I have been searching for you in great anxiety" (Luke 2:48).

The response of the twelve-year-old boy was to say, "Why were you searching for me? Did you not know that I must be in my Father's house?" Seems as though he was playing by different rules from his parents'. As it turns out, Luke tells us, "then he went down with them and came to Nazareth, and was obedient to them" (Luke 2:49-51). I take this to mean that he accepted the rules laid down by his parents.

Before there are rules for games, there are rules for living. Before a child discovers toys, she discovers rules. The child's schedule of eating and sleeping is quickly regulated to fit into the "rules" of the household. Nighttime is for sleeping and daytime is for being awake— that's the rule! "No," the child is told, "we don't throw our food." "No, you may not hit your brother."

When visiting our daughter, I took my grandson Brandon out for a walk. We were about to escape the narrow confines of the sidewalk and stroll happily down the street when an adult member of my family ran to us and warned me, "Brandon can only be in the street when he's holding your hand." The purpose of that rule was to keep him from running into the street on his own.

Sure enough, as soon as I put out my hand, Brandon took it. He knew the rule well enough, but seeing that I didn't know it, he pretended it didn't exist. He would have preferred being in the street without having to be constrained by an adult, but apparently he was willing to accept the rule for the sake of gaining access to an otherwise forbidden place.

The Double Bind of Rules and Relationships

Most—if not all—children are not happy about a rule when they first encounter it. Thus rules may well come to be associated with unhappiness, and freedom from rules with happiness. In this case I mean by happiness the unbridled freedom of self-expression, which, as we have seen in the previous chapter, is experienced as a fulfillment of the pleasure instinct.

Rules are not innate boundaries and checks against self-expression; they are learned from others. Rules and relationships are therefore bound together in a kind of paradox.

Relationships are necessary and essential to the longing of the self for fulfillment and pleasure. True happiness is possible only when this longing is fulfilled and we experience relationship to others. At the same time, constraints in the form of rules are introduced by others in the context of these primary relationships. This is the double bind of rules and relationships.

I have no recollection of what happened to the relationship I had with my opponent in the aborted game of marbles. Being the competitive person that I am, I can only guess that I learned to shoot well enough with my fist on the ground to come back and beat him by his own rules. One lesson I learned as a child seems to have been, If you don't like the rules set by others, don't play; but if you do, play to win! I also discovered, however, that this does not contribute to one's happiness in life.

If the child resolves the double bind of rules and relationships by suppressing joy for the sake of conformity to the rules, this preserves the relationship with the person who set the rules. The relationship, however, then tends to be primarily rule-oriented. The one who sets the rules has the power to punish disobedience and deny access to the child's only source of security and comfort.

At this point, a splitting of the self can occur. The "happy self" withdraws into the child's own world, where imagination creates its own rules, sometimes peopled with imaginary playmates who play by their creator's rules. The "unhappy self," devoid of real joy, accepts the terms of relationships by conformity to the rules. On the surface an effective adjustment seems to have been made, with the caregiver and rule-maker taking compliance as obedience. This splitting between an unhappy and a happy self can lead to chronic unhappiness in an adult. Long before that, it can even lead to serious personality disorder in the child if it isn't resolved.

Arnold is a friend and former student. As our paths cross from time to time, we share stories of mutual pain and pleasure. Most recently his story has been one of deep dissatisfaction with his life. He thinks he might be experiencing burnout, or at least the symptoms of midlife crisis. Both are apparently acceptable terms, giving social permission to vent unhappiness while preserving some semblance of dignity.

Arnold is a dutiful father and tries to fulfill his responsibilities as a husband by following the rules. When he's reminded of these rules, as he sometimes tends to become lax, he makes new efforts to conform. In his professional life he has success by emphasizing his creative gifts and people-pleasing skills. But this success, though it is personally gratifying, doesn't reinforce his family and professional relationships. Not only do these relationships not give him the same gratification as his work, but he tends to become estranged and nonfunctional. Generally he functions best when he can set the rules. This pattern has led to several vocational changes and moves. He is currently trying to resolve a relationship crisis by considering another job change.

As we talk, I sense that as an adult Arnold is still tormented by the unresolved issue of his "happy child" and his "unhappy child." Forced by a rather dysfunctional family system to pull himself up by his own bootstraps, he lived within the rules but played beyond them. He accepted the traditional roles of marriage and professional life but kept his "happy child" sufficiently free to be nurtured and gratified by his more creative gifts.

The successes he creates and the gratification he receives at one level only compound the unhappiness and lack of fulfillment he feels in living by other people's rules. His unhappiness is pervasive and chronic, alleviated only by the dreams he lives out in short-term successes. He finds it difficult to communicate his feelings of happiness with those who are in primary relationships with him, either in his family or in his professional world. He is disengaged from others by his happiness and related to them only by his unhappiness. He is caught in the double bind of rules and relationships.

Like Arnold, many people find it difficult to integrate experiences that make them feel good about themselves with the day-by-day routine of life. I believe that we learn this kind of unhappiness in our childhood. If we feel that rules are arbitrary and lead to a loss of the happiness that we experience as playful pleasure, we associate rules with unhappiness. Because rules are what connects us to those on whom we depend for our daily doses of comfort and security, a pervasive unhappiness can develop when we feel our freedom unjustly constrained by rules. If we were to throw off the rules, we would lose the relationships we need.

Those Pesky Rules

Let me describe an unhappy adult and how that unhappiness might have been learned as a child for whom rules were wrongly used to control behavior.

For the child, the regular and routine functions of dressing, eating, sleeping and even playing are defined by rules set by someone else. This is true in every case. A love that did not know how and when to apply rules would not be true love. What we want to explore here is the *wrong* use of rules, even when they are grounded in motivations that are felt to be love.

When the child experiences rules without a connection with the deeper longings of the self for fulfillment and pleasure, the rules become arbitrary boundaries. In this case the rules not only set limits but also deny the reality of the self's longing for fulfillment. In the words of an old song, the self essentially longs to sing, "I gotta be me!"

If this should happen, we may seek to escape from the rules by either withdrawing to an inner life of our own or intentionally crossing over the boundaries set for us. Only then do we regain the feeling of pleasure and feel happy.

The two-year-old who slips away from a parent's grasp and runs headlong for the green grass on the other side of the street has surrendered to the irresistible urge for a pleasure forbidden by the rules. The fact that the child has suddenly become deaf to the parent's frantic calls only indicates how all-consuming is the aroused pleasure instinct. What the child hears with the ears is not as compelling as what inspires the imagination. Of course the parent finally catches up and the adventure is over. The parent's fear for the child's safety is expressed in words that sound like anger to the child. The strong arms that subdue the child's frantic struggles to get free feel harsh and unyielding. It is not a pleasant feeling.

The lure of the green grass and the pleasure of the headlong rush toward it promised joy but have now resulted in disapproval. The actions that give pleasure and speak to this unspoken longing are not permitted. More than that, the very feelings that led to the breaking of the rules are now judged to be wrong and unacceptable. When parents use words like "you are a naughty boy to do that," the child may not understand the precise meaning, but he or she receives the negative message clearly enough and internalizes a judgment against the happy self. Soon enough the child will learn that *naughty* means "bad" and that *good* means doing only what is permitted.

For the unhappy adult, the lesson learned through repeated episodes of breaking the rules and being caught is that we are connected by feelings of unhappiness to those who have the power to control our lives. Because these connections are regular and routine, we grow up with the assurance that this is "normal." Unhappiness is the price we are expected to pay for the benefits of a warm bed, regular meals and the approval of society. We receive the reward of being loved if we are "good." This again is the double bind. To receive love we must "pay our dues" and live by the rules, even at the cost of our happiness.

For those adults who grew up in this way, happiness is experienced privately and clandestinely. The repressed longing for fulfillment and joy becomes the secret of the self, disguised so as not to appear threatening to those whose tyranny over us is justified by their certainty that the rules are for our good and it is done only because they love us. No one rules over us more tyrannically, someone once said, than those who say that they only want to love us!

My friend Arnold has a "normal" marriage and family, with a quite respectable track record in his professional field. His résumé is impressive, and he has achieved recognition far beyond his home office. At the same time he tells me, "The personal expectations of those with whom I live and work make me feel like a failure. I feel that I am always on trial or that I have failed in some essential aspect of my relationships. I long for the kind of appreciation and response from my family and from my coworkers that I get from individuals who know me best for my contribution toward their lives."

Arnold does not receive what he "longs for" from those who set the rules for his life. These rules are not arbitrary, and he has willingly contracted for them in entering into marriage, becoming a parent and joining a professional team in the workplace. His happiness is not found in these relationships as much as when he has the freedom to be by himself, with no strings attached.

At home Arnold has a hobby room where he can retreat from the family and escape into his own world, where no one can make demands on him. At work he cuts loose from the routine to spend time alone at a favorite restaurant or coffee shop; it's there that he does his creative thinking and works on designing new products. No one would accuse Arnold of having a "double life," but in fact he does. He has a happy life that belongs to his private world and an unhappy life at both home and work.

In his creative gifts and skills, which produce materials that are valued by those who use them, he finds immense pleasure and self-fulfillment. But these times and experiences of happiness take place outside his role as husband, father and team player. He is like a high-wire performer in the circus, trying to keep his balance by holding up his unhappy commitments with one hand and reaching out with the other hand for the experiences that nourish his soul with happiness. No wonder he feels close to burnout! The emotional energy required to keep his act together is tremendous.

One possible source of chronic unhappiness in adults is a learned pattern of feelings associated with rules that feel like arbitrary con-straints on one's freedom. As I have indicated, when this becomes a more or less predictable emotional response of the self—even to self-imposed commitments and responsibilities—unhappiness settles in like a dreary winter of discontent.

This kind of unhappiness is puzzling and frustrating because it is not caused by events that intrude into one's life. It is not the result of bad luck or even foolish choices. It would be easier if one could account for unhappiness by pointing to an overdraft at the bank, a car breakdown after the warranty has run out or an unkind word from a close friend. When we get over our shock and disappointment, most of these kinds of things can be fixed or resolved.

The unhappiness that results from the splitting of the happy self from the rules of normal relationships cannot be fixed so easily. When the unhappiness becomes apparent to others, it is usually in the form of a breakdown in family relationships or the work environment. The one who has failed to function effectively is at a loss and makes new promises to change behavior in order to meet the demands of others.

But these efforts are undermined by their failure to produce happiness. A new level of failure is introduced, and the unhappiness spreads like a virus through the relational system. A dysfunctional relationship cannot fix itself. Professional counseling is suggested, and the unhappiness is carried to the therapist's office like dirty laundry to the laundromat when the washer at home has broken down.

Arnold has been through counseling. It was not his idea but was part of the deal he made with his family to resolve problems that he felt were largely due to his inability to meet his wife's expectations. He had no clue why he felt reluctance from the very beginning. He tried not to let it show, but in the end the therapist concluded the counseling with the suggestion that Arnold was resistant to the process.

An unhappy person's resistance to counseling should not surprise us. The core motivation of the self is linked to the longing for joy, not to the virtue of duty. There may be rewards for doing one's duty, but pleasure is not usually one of them. Indeed, when we have found some sense of fulfillment and joy outside of our structured duty, it's hard to let go of that pleasure for the sake of a joyless responsibility. We shouldn't be expected to starve the happy child to feed the unhappy one.

The unhappy child cannot be made to do what is impossible—to be happy. Only the happy child can lead us back to the place where the rules can be integrated with happiness.

Letting the Child Lead

When I took Brandon's hand to go to the street, his father captured the scene with a video camera. I watched the tape recently and noticed that I began to walk down the street in one direction. After a few steps Brandon pulled in the other direction, and I, having no clear itinerary for our stroll, followed. As we pursued our way back down the street, his attention was caught by a Jeep parked across the street. This Jeep was of a military type, without a top. As we drew near the Jeep, he dropped my hand and reached up to climb into it. I helped him into the seat, and he grasped the wheel with both hands and "steered" it with gusto. Then, abruptly stopping, he reached back with one hand and pulled the seat belt forward. He had learned another rule in the family car and now was able to transfer it to his "own car."

As I reflected on this experience, I discovered an insight into the apparent double bind between rules and relationships. At first glance the rule "Brandon cannot go into the street without holding your hand" appeared arbitrary and designed to restrict his freedom. Even I felt that it was a confining, albeit necessary, rule.

But Brandon taught me something and learned something for himself. When I allowed him to lead me to explore the adventure of sitting in the Jeep, the rule became associated with that which fulfilled his longing and made him happy. The rule didn't mean that I should always determine the direction of our walk, but only that he should hold my hand. Just because I was stronger and supposedly wiser in the ways of the world, I did not have a right to apply the rule to suit my own pleasure. The rule, after all, was meant not only for his safety but also for his pleasure. When we applied the rule in such a way that he experienced some fulfillment of what he longed for, it no longer evoked a negative feeling of unhappiness.

I had never thought about rules in that way before. Each and every rule cannot bring about a pleasurable experience. But self-identity is often formed through relationship to persons to which rules can become attached. This results in the formation of an internal self-identity that becomes the core of the person.

In a healthy parent-child relationship, periods of separation are necessary to establish continuity and the child's positive sense of self. The caregiver, as the one through whom the child begins to form core self-identity, cannot always be with the child. During these times of separation, the child may become panicked and uncertain. But when the two are reunited, positive self-identity is maintained. Eventually the child can experience times of separation calmly.

Rules too can have a positive effect when they lead to a shared experience in which the child receives affirmation and self-fulfillment. Sometimes the child will experience rules as limiting and arbitrary. But there must be enough continuity in the basic rules for the child to associate them with happiness. This means that some rules must allow the child to lead and the adult to participate in the child's happiness. When this experience is repeated over time, the child begins to develop a positive association between rules and happiness. Both belong to the regular and routine structures of life.

The day after the Jeep incident, Brandon and I went outside to get into the family car for a short trip. Once again he reached for my hand and headed for the Jeep. This time I simply said, "No, Brandon, we'll do that when we get back." He was obviously disappointed, but he allowed himself to be placed in the car, and we drove off. In this case the rule was applied without regard to his immediate pleasure, with firmness and no basis for appeal.

But I must remember the promise, even if Brandon doesn't. For there must be a "next time" when the rule is applied for the sake of his pleasure.

When a deep core of happiness is formed in the self, unhappiness can fade away without a trace. But when unhappiness is the prevailing feeling of the self, happiness has no roots. It is like cut flowers taken out of the garden and placed in a vase.

My friend Arnold will need to reconnect with the happiness that has become dissociated from his primary network of relationships and reexperience the "hand-in-hand" rule that permits him to lead the way and others to participate. This will not be an easy process. There are no shortcuts. However it takes place, it must be with someone who can release the empowerment potential in his happy self to receive the rules of daily life and be nourished in his soul where he is constrained by love.

Arnold is a grown man, not a little boy. This is why he resisted "taking the hand" of the therapist, even though his wife desperately wanted him to help work on their dysfunctional relationship. As I once did, he picked up his marbles and went home.

I suggested that he approach his family using the analogy of a game of marbles: they could make up a new game for which each member could help create the rules. He tried the suggestion. It began with a planned weekly outing; several meetings were held to work out the "rules" for the outing in such a way that each family member could anticipate some pleasure in the activity. Arnold and his wife could thus begin to attach rules to pleasure rather than to each other.

Shared pleasure following agreed-upon rules is the beginning of happiness. For Arnold, the potential for happiness was there; he only needed to learn how to release it.

Of Birds and Rocky Soil
Jesus spoke eloquently to this point when he told the parable of the sower (Matthew 13). The seed that fell on the pathway was immediately eaten by birds; the seed that fell on rocky soil lacked roots and withered when the hot sun appeared; the seed that fell on soil filled with weeds was soon choked by the other plants and died; the seed that fell on the "good soil" prospered and brought forth an abundant harvest.

When Jesus interpreted this parable to his disciples, he likened the soil to the person who receives the good news of the kingdom of God. There are three kinds of "unhappiness" according to the parable but only one kind of "happiness." There are many reasons persons are unable to receive and thrive in the goodness and grace of God. As Tolstoy wrote in the opening lines of *Anna Karenina*, all happy marriages are the same but each unhappy marriage is unhappy in its own way.

The two kinds of unhappiness we have examined thus far correspond to the seed sown on the pathway and that sown in rocky soil. The unhappiness that results from needing to possess the right kind of toy leads to a feeling that life is not fair, for what you already possess can be taken from you and someone else has what you want. The birds of unhappiness are always circling overhead to pluck the seeds we scatter on the pathway of life.

The unhappiness that comes from experiencing the rules of life as denying our pleasure leads to a feeling that life is not freeing, for rules appear to force us to live in relationships that are confining and sterile. The rocky soil of unhappiness causes the tender plants of our deepest longings for freedom to wither and perish.

There is also a third kind of unhappiness. This comes from a feeling of always being on the losing end. The competition is severe and unceasing. For many, life is a marathon with little hope of winning and a good deal of concern about finishing. Life is not friendly for the unhappy person, and in the next chapter we will seek to find the reason.

3

Someone Else
Always Gets
First Place:
Life Is Not Friendly

*T*he halftime show for a recent nationally televised football game included a crawling race between eight little girls under two years of age. After each of the girls was presented by her football-player father, they were set in place and started on their way. The child who reached the finish line first was awarded first place.

From what I could see, all of the girls who participated were just as happy as the one who received first prize. The father of the winning girl, however, clearly exceeded the other fathers in his exuberance. He had learned how important it is to win. The football coach credited with first stating this competitive adage has since fired up hundreds of others: "Winning isn't the most important thing—it's the only thing!"

From beautiful baby contests, to crawling contests, to spelling bees, to Little League baseball, to teen beauty pageants, to Scholastic Aptitude Tests and college entrance tests, to competitive criteria for job placement and promotion, people are pressured to win. This cultural craze for competition begins as early as preschool and continues throughout the educational process. It begins with the ruthless competition for highest grades in school and continues in competitive sports, even as vicariously experienced in family living rooms culminating with Super Bowl Sunday. Not a few family gatherings have suddenly turned sour when the favorite team loses a critical game.

The Joy of Friendly Competition

In friendly competition there are winners and losers, but no one is robbed of dignity and left humiliated and wounded. Here the competitors are each competing primarily within themselves to do their best and only secondarily with someone else. There is a realistic assessment of one's own capability alongside that of others. Often the challenge is to discover the extent of one's skill and capability in a fierce but fair competition.

The apostle Paul was not above calling our attention to the competitive nature of life when he said, "Do you not know that in a race the runners all compete, but only one receives the prize? Run in such a way that you may win it" (1 Corinthians 9:24). He went on to testify to his own drive to win: "So I do not run aimlessly, nor do I box as though beating the air; but I punish my body and enslave it, so that after proclaiming to others I myself should not be disqualified" (vv. 26-27).

What are we to make of this? Does God hold out a prize for the winners in life and turn away the losers with nothing? Does Paul mean to say that if one crowds out the others in order to win, that person has gained something in the end? Hardly. Paul used the race metaphor to stress the importance of self-discipline in order to achieve self-chosen goals. No one has to lose, for the race is not against others, but for the prize.

Not long ago I watched a televised broadcast of another sporting event. It was a Special Olympics foot race run by persons who suffered from various forms of handicap. Contestants who were mentally or physically handicapped ran as best they could around the track. Suddenly one among them fell. As if on cue, the others stopped running and went back to help him up. When he was back on his feet, off they went again, "competing" with one another to win the race.

The Bible seems to have something to say about this as well. "Two are better than one, because they have a good reward for their toil. For if they fall, one will lift up the other; but woe to one who is alone and falls and does not have another to help" (Ecclesiastes 4:9-10).

When we become adults, we are less prone to risk our dignity and race our desires as boldly as when we were young. For one thing, we have learned to avoid win-lose encounters, for no one likes to be a loser. At the same time many of us carry a smoldering grievance that has no connection with our current conflicts. While we do not compete as much as we once did, something deep within us feels the shame of losing.

When we have given our all in a contest and haven't come in first, it's healthy to grieve the loss of the goal that we didn't attain. This is a grief that, when healed, makes us stronger and more resilient. It is quite another thing for a grief to become a grievance and for our pain to become split off from the event that caused it.

Not all competitive experiences in life are friendly. This is especially true when the adult level of competition intrudes on children. Left to themselves, children struggle with each other to be first in almost every encounter. This need is rooted in the longing for self-fulfillment, which I discussed in the first two chapters as the basis for the pleasure instinct. When this longing is expressed through a competitive encounter, the stakes are high. The loss of first place is like a stab of pain back into the center of the self. The child retreats and looks for another opportunity to gain the recognition that is essential to a sense of well-being.

This recognition can come through a variety of forms. The child's loss to the self in one encounter can quickly be made up by a special hug from her parent, with the assurance that she always has "first place" in that relationship. The place of children in family relationships is meant, in a sense, to equalize competitive gains and losses. Both winners and losers in the games children invent to challenge each other go home with deeper needs for belonging than any game can give. For all the flush of victory that quickens the pulse, there is a deeper longing that winning cannot fulfill.

When adult-level competition intrudes on the lives of children, there is no longer the equalizer of childhood dependence on caregiving adults. The children are exposed to the same win-at-all-cost attitude as adults. The children wear miniature models of adult uniforms and emulate their adult heroes in mannerisms, language and contempt for losers. When these children go home they take the game with them, and the conversation at the dinner table is replete with bravado and threats. The anxious parent, upset by the suffering of a child whose team has lost, will say, "Don't worry, next week when we play them we'll get even. We'll pound them into the ground—we'll show them up for the crybabies they are!"

Losing Hurts Bitterly

I have no recollection of winning a spelling contest in elementary school, but the one that I lost floods back on me in an instant when I open the door to that memory. The embarrassment of the long walk back to my desk cut like a knife to the core of my being. The triumphant look on the face of the schoolmate who won by spelling the word correctly added salt to my wound.

Later, when my mother asked how I had done in the contest, I mumbled something about how stupid it was and I really didn't care who won. Not to care was my way of handling a loss, for if I cared too much it hurt too much.

Every one of us has experienced the unhappiness of losing a contest, whether it was an argument, a graded assignment or a game of skill. We can't idealize children's playtime as blissfully innocent when we watch their pushing and shoving to be first. For every winner there is a small crowd of losers. If the tears dry quickly and a new game is invented, we should not be surprised to discover that the unhappiness of losing is often carried home as a silent witness to an aching loss.

Losing not only hurts, it hurts bitterly. It is how we cope with the bitter unhappiness of losing that is the key to our emotional and spiritual well-being as adults.

When we are exposed to the emotional trauma of competition, which has the power to rob us of dignity and leave us embarrassed and defeated, the grievance against life gains its hold on the inner life of the self. We can only hate the winner for so long. Retaliation against those who defeated us is beyond the powers of most of us. Long after we forget who it was that took first and robbed us of our place in the sun, we carry the grievance of that loss. A vague sense that life itself is our combatant and that we will always lose out begins to take hold of us. We have now become unhappy adults, and no win is big enough to offset our loss.

The chronic unhappiness of many adults can be traced directly back to childhood experiences in which someone robbed them of the recognition and affirmation they were desperately seeking by "coming in first." I use the term *robbed* deliberately, for it is exactly this sense of having something stolen from us by someone else that produces our deeply felt grievance in losing.

The one who comes in first when we have set our hearts on that goal steals what we already have claimed as ours. If losing were only a personal failure, that would be sufficient to plunge us into unhappiness. We might berate ourselves for failing but not carry a grievance against the one who won.

But there are some losses that are perceived as a violation of our right of being. The one who gains first place steals the recognition we feel we deserve. When losing results in feelings of humiliation and unworthiness, we feel violated, stripped of something so important that no consolation can make up for its loss. The shame of losing turns to a rage and desire for retaliation against the one who has done this to us.

The humiliation of losing quickly gives way to a deep-seated grievance against the one who has stolen the prize we desperately desired. This is a kind of unhappiness different from the temporary feeling of loss that comes through failure. This is a toxic unhappiness that poisons the well from which we drink daily. The moments of happiness that come from other pleasures fall into this well and, when drawn back up, have the bitter taste of unhappiness in them.

When Unhappiness Turns Deadly

One of the oldest stories in the Bible describes how the malady of unhappiness is connected with the misery of losing out in a competition. The result was fatal. The two sons of Adam and Eve were apparently well schooled in the necessity of seeking God's favor through an offering. Abel, we are told, was a keeper of sheep and Cain a tiller of the ground. "In the course of time Cain brought to the LORD an offering of the fruit of the ground, and Abel for his part brought of the firstlings of his flock, their fat portions. And the LORD had regard for Abel and his offering, but for Cain and his offering he had no regard" (Genesis 4:3-5).

Note that the regard of the Lord was for Abel himself, not only for his offering. Likewise, the disfavor of the Lord was toward Cain and his offering. What is gained and lost are not only religious merit points on a game scorecard but also a sense of the worth and value of one's own self. Cain was angry, we are told, and his countenance fell. To Cain the Lord said, "Why are you angry, and why has your countenance fallen? If you do well, will you not be accepted? And if you do not do well, sin is lurking at the door; its desire is for you, but you must master it" (vv. 6-7).

A vicious desire for retaliation prompted Cain from within, urging him to strike out in anger against this apparent injustice. This is what I have called "toxic unhappiness." It is a grievance against the one who has gained first place and secured the recognition that the self earnestly desired and sought. This feeling is irrational, of course, and does not consider that this was not a contest between Cain and his brother, with only one winner allowed. Fueled by the longing for happiness that was now denied, this desperate desire became a fury of unhappiness ready to be unleashed against his brother. As it turned out, Cain soon found an opportunity to kill Abel and spilled his blood on the ground, from which it cried out to God (vv. 8-10).

This story suggests to us that there is a primal unhappiness that underlies all competition. What may begin as friendly jousting suddenly turns deadly serious, and someone gets hurt. Rather than competition itself being the source of brutality and violence, it is the deadly desire of unhappiness that has a "score to settle."

Are we born with the grievance of Cain flowing through our natal blood? Is there a virus that produces violence, a virus that waits for any provocation to attack our unsuspecting brothers and sisters? Is this the alien from within the human race that is projected on the alien from outer space that our movies portray with such horrifying impact? In an insightful analysis of the human propensity toward betrayal and violence, the playwright Arthur Miller says, "We are very dangerous. . . . The wish to kill is never killed, but with some gift of courage one may look into its face when it appears, and with a stroke of love—as to an idiot in the house—forgive it; again and again . . ."

William Golding, in his classic *The Lord of the Flies,* describes in dramatic detail the social and psychological disintegration of childhood innocence into savage brutality and horror with a group of boys shipwrecked on a deserted island. Their competitive playfulness soon escalated into a highly organized and deadly game of terror. What was meant to be a parable of our own chaotic times may well be a modern commentary on the primal unhappiness injected into the human race as described in the Cain and Abel story.

No longer can we dismiss unhappiness as an "unhealthy attitude" for which the cure is repeated doses of manufactured pleasure. The toxic unhappiness that carries a grievance is not due to a pleasure deficiency for which a joy vitamin pill can be prescribed. This kind of unhappiness leads to violence against children by their own parents and the abuse of one spouse by another.

Apparently we all carry the seed of this unhappiness. The pushing and shoving for first place among children infects their playful competition. They reveal a primitive desire to get even for ancient losses when they crow over victories and humiliate losers. Gang wars range over an urban battlefield where grown-up children fight a deadly game with real bullets. Revenge and retaliation ignite new fires out of the ashes of yesterday's combat losses.

With sufficient restraint, most children survive the first round and move into their adulthood having learned, as Miller wrote, to acknowledge this "wish to kill" and submit it to the "stroke of love." Some simply become more proficient in making out of this toxic unhappiness a clever skill for manipulation and control of others. Such skill is amply rewarded in a society where success and power are worshiped for their own sake.

But there are many others—some of whom I meet in the counseling room—whose toxic unhappiness has turned inward and whose bitterness is unleashed with pitiless scorn against their own selves. These unhappy adults feel choked and strangled by life, like the seed planted in soil filled with weeds in the parable Jesus told (Matthew 13). The desire to retaliate is still present, but is deflected back onto the self.

Occasionally those who become caught up in our toxic unhappiness receive the blows. Even if this does not include verbal or physical violence, the living space becomes fouled with the emotional discharge of our noxious grievance.

Receiving the Stroke of Love

Arthur Miller's turn of phrase catches my eye. "The wish to kill is never killed, but with some gift of courage one may look into its face when it appears, and with a stroke of love—as to an idiot in the house—forgive it; again and again." I want to know more about this stroke of love.

I return to the story of Cain and Abel. There I read that God spoke lovingly and compassionately to Cain. "Why are you angry, and why has your countenance fallen? If you do well, will you not be accepted? And if you do not do well, sin is lurking at the door; its desire is for you, but you must master it" (Genesis 4:6-7). God did not try to cheer Cain up. Behind Cain's "fallen countenance," which we may take to be an expression of abject disappointment and probably an obvious sulk, God pointed to the anger. I have called it a grievance. In any event, God gave the "stroke of love" to Cain by cutting through to the bare bone of his unhappiness with surgical skill. There was also an incredible promise of acceptance and the intimation that Cain had the resources to "master" the situation and regain control of himself. God's stroke of love bared the arm of God's forgiveness, reaching out to touch the fear and stroke the fury of Cain's hurting heart.

For reasons hidden from humanity from that day until now, Cain fought off that divine love, proceeded to plot revenge against his brother and soon found opportunity to slay him. If Miller was right, it wasn't enough for Cain to receive the stroke of God's love; he needed to *give himself* the stroke of love, acknowledge that he was "very dangerous" and forgive within himself that terrible desire to take vengeance on another for his loss. God's stroke sought to touch in Cain a response of love—toward God, toward his brother and toward himself. If only we knew how to love ourselves.

I think here of David, the king of Israel who allowed his desire to take by force Bathsheba, the wife of Uriah, one of his army officers. When David found out that Bathsheba was pregnant, he tried to cover up his wrong by giving her husband a weekend pass. When that plan failed, he arranged to have Uriah killed in battle (2 Samuel 11). As a consequence, the child born to Bathsheba died, and David was faced with the enormous pain of what he had done. He received God's "stroke of love" from Nathan the prophet, who exposed the wrong but at the same assured him of God's continued love (2 Samuel 12).

Can David give the stroke of love to himself and forgive himself? In a psalm of confession, David wrote, "Create in me a clean heart, O God, and put a new and right spirit within me. . . . Restore to me the joy of your salvation, and sustain in me a willing spirit" (Psalm 51:10, 12). David did acknowledge that the source of his unhappiness was within himself: "Indeed, I was born guilty, a sinner when my mother conceived me" (v. 5). He was then empowered to forgive and give himself the stroke of love.

In considering the form of unhappiness that arises from the natal grievance called original sin, we discover the need for a stroke of love from a gracious God that uncovers this fatal and deadly motive within us. Despite our unhappiness, we may consider ourselves lucky and momentarily happy if our spirit of vengeance and hatred toward others has not been discovered. But this is a false sense of happiness. True happiness arises when the pernicious problem in us is discovered and exposed by the kind of love and grace that only God can show.

The failure of Cain to make this move staggers us with the shocking reality of the power of this toxic unhappiness to resist even God's grace. But the story of Cain is not a final verdict against the possibility of love. It is, rather, a reminder to us that "we are very dangerous," and that left to ourselves we would perish in our pain and self-pity.

It really hurts to lose. It hurts bitterly. And when we hurt, no one hurts more than we do. Perhaps we can't give ourselves the stroke of love because it still hurts too much, and the child within us, bruised and battered, still recoils from the outstretched arm of love. This hurt must be attended to if happiness is to grow in the good soil of love and grace.

4

When I'm Hurt, No One Feels As Bad As I Do

I was in my teens. I sat on the edge of the family circle, nursing some grievance. When someone commented on my lack of participation, my mother responded, "Don't mind Ray—he's just got his feelings hurt!"

The remark did not have a therapeutic effect, though it was a common enough expression in those days. I suppose suffering attributed to hurt feelings was thought to be like the common cold: there was no cure for it, but we were expected to get over it in a few days.

In retrospect, *hurt feelings* is a curious expression. What are "feelings," and how can they be "hurt"? We feel pain when injured, and we say "it hurts" when the doctor applies pressure to a sore spot on the body. The days of our childhood were filled with flurries of feelings, most of which seem to have disappeared without a trace, like a frown that suffers a meltdown in the face of a smile.

But there are feelings in every child that hurt beyond the telling; these painful feelings become the taut strand on which the pearls of memory are strung. Some of these memory pearls are misshapen and ugly. We may attempt to remove them or to heal them, but until the strand of hurt feelings itself is repaired, we will not experience abiding happiness.

When my feelings are hurt, I hurt from the inside out. There is no scrape on the knee or cut on the finger that I can point to when someone says, "Let me kiss it and make it feel better!" When my feelings are hurt, I know that no one else in all the world feels as bad as I do. I feel the cut, the stab and the stinging pain. The throb of hurt feelings is impervious to the analgesic remedies offered by well-meaning persons who seek to cheer us up.

The kind of unhappiness that comes from hurt feelings may look like self-pity to others, but it feels like crucifixion to the one who is hurting. "If you are the Son of God, come down from the cross," some passersby shouted at the dying Jesus (Matthew 27:40). They were implying that he could get out of his predicament if he "really wanted to." "Just leave him alone," they say when we won't dance at their party or join their parade. "He'll join us when he feels like it." They don't realize that we carry the childhood affliction called "hurt feelings" that flares up at the slightest provocation.

The Care and Feeding of Our Feelings
Feelings may be the most critical indicators of well-being that we possess. The feelings we acquire as infants and children form the matrix of the self for our adult years. Feelings need care and nurture as much as, if not more than, the physical parts of the self. When our feelings are sick, there is no health in us. Without feelings we have no contact with the world and no relationship with others.

The infant's earliest responses to another person's attention do not always require touch. The infant experiences itself under the stimulation of smells, sounds and visual images as well as touch. The core of the self in the infant actively responds to the self of another and is experienced as feelings. Infants can actually *feel* the presence of another without being touched. These feelings are not merely sensations that the self has, as though there were an unfeeling self hidden behind the responsive self. The feelings *are* the self, and the capacity to respond to the presence of another is the capacity to feel. This response means growth for the self when the other's presence is loving and caring.

Feelings are an essential and accurate expression of the self, says Archibald Hart, professor of psychology at the Fuller Seminary Graduate School of Psychology. Many consider *feelings* and *emotions* synonymous, but they are not. Our emotions may be distorted when we make incorrect interpretations of what we experience, but feelings are connected directly to the self and serve as a guide to restoring the unity and health of the self.

Because love is attributed to God as the essence of divine motivation and action, it is also the core expression of the image of God in human beings. Love is not only an act of volition, says the theologian Emil Brunner, but it is an expression of *feeling.*

Feeling therefore has its rightful place in man's "experience" of his relation with God, because this "experience" is something which man has received, and not something which he has created. To be apprehended by the love of God, means to be smitten in the very centre of one's being, to suffer it, not as pain, but as the supreme joy, as happiness and peace; that is, the Self knows that it is "at home" in God, and that the "I" and the "Self" have become one.

To the Western mind with its European bent toward the abstract, feelings and intellect are assumed to be separate parts of the self. Feelings, and therefore experience, are discounted as subjective and unreliable. In the biblical perspective, however, feelings are located at the core of the self in its orientation toward God and the other.

With the fall into sin, the original unity of feeling with love and knowledge was severed, resulting in the psychological separation of feeling from the spirit. The severance of pleasure from relation to God left the intrinsic drive for self-fulfillment frustrated and unfulfilled. As a result, self-gratification became an insatiable substitute for happiness. The connection between feelings and the core of the self's longing for fulfillment needs to be reestablished.

When feelings, as the response capacity of the self, are nurtured and encouraged, touch can also produce the feeling of happiness and pleasure. The self longs for fulfillment; this is the basis for the pleasure-seeking instinct. When pleasure is reinforced, infants begin to develop a sense of the self and a capacity to interpret the sense-experience phenomena of life as either pleasant or unpleasant. This is a lifelong process.

Who knows what the feelings of pain and pleasure are like for the child too young to remember and tell us? The infant cries when hungry, hurt or fearful. At least we associate the tears with the circumstances that seem to cause them. The philosopher John Macmurray said there are body sensations for pain but not for pleasure. Feelings of pleasure, he suggested, are not the result of sensation alone but originate in the self's capacity to interpret sensation as feelings of pleasure. The same touch that produces a feeling of pleasure, if continued, will soon become uncomfortable and begin to feel painful.

When called names as a child, we learned to respond with the taunt "Sticks and stones can break my bones, but words can never hurt me." Wrong! We *felt* the blow of unkind words at the very core of our being, and even now we carry above or below consciousness the anger, shame and humiliation caused by words said to us with intent to hurt.

Feelings Lie Close to the Heart

Feelings are more than sensations produced by external stimuli. Feelings are more than emotions that flood the terrain of the inner self. Feelings *are* the self as a living and experiencing being. Where the self exists, feelings are present, even if unrecognized or unexpressed.

In the diary of a girl not yet twelve, named Opal by her foster parents, the precocious thoughts of a child who experienced her self as "feeling" surprise us with their clarity and truth:

Now are come the days of leaves.
They talk with the wind.
I hear them tell of their borning days.
They whisper of the hoods they wear.
Today they talk of the time
before their borning days.
They tell how they were part of the earth
and the air before their tree-borning days.
In grey days of winter
they go back to earth again.
But they do not die.
I saw a silken cradle in a hazel branch.
It was cream with a hazel leaf
halfway around it.
I put it to my ear and I did listen.
It had a little voice.
It was a heart voice.
While I did listen, I did feel its feels.
It has lovely ones.
I did hurry to the house of the girl
who has no seeing
so she might know its feels
and hear its heart voice.
She does so like to feel things.
She has seeing by feels.

Feelings are like an iceberg; nine-tenths of them may lie below the surface of consciousness. We may think that we have no feelings or that we have our feelings under control, but then we find ourselves reacting and acting in ways that betray the power of these submerged feelings. Opal, who lost both parents at the age of five and was placed in the home of a family working the Oregon lumber camps at the turn of the century, cultivated her experience of self. She did it with respect to her world of animals, trees and flowers at a depth of feeling that threatened to burst through her limited vocabulary like a geyser. "While I did listen," she tells us, "I did feel its feels."

What psychologists call "the unconscious" may be feelings that cannot be directly identified by the self at the conscious, or cognitive, level. These "unconscious" feelings often come to expression in our behavior without any "logical" explanation. Or they may appear in symbolic form in our dreams. We can experience these depth feelings even though we may never be able to think about them or communicate them to others.

For example, all of us have had experiences that have a certain mystical quality about them. I have had a sense of being "moonstruck" when the immensity and power of a moonbeam slicing through the night seemed to be aimed right at the core of my being, connecting me with some invisible and intangible reality I could not explain. People have been known to weep at the playing of a single note from a childhood tune long forgotten. Lovers tremble and friends fall silent in the sudden and incredible shock of the presence of the *other*, as though a curtain has been lifted momentarily and the undiluted spirit of another soul breathes on us. When one of the first astronauts orbited the earth and looked out at the slowly spinning globe that he called home, he had an experience so deeply personal and spiritual that it transformed his life forever.

The apostle Paul, overwhelmed on the road to Damascus by the reality of a resurrected Jesus Christ, wrote of an experience of God that crosses over the boundary that divides our feeling self from our perceiving self. Citing the words of the prophet Isaiah (found in Isaiah 64:4), Paul wrote, " 'What no eye has seen, nor ear heard, nor the human heart conceived, what God has prepared for those who love him'—these things God has revealed to us through the Spirit; for the Spirit searches everything, even the depths of God" (1 Corinthians 2:9-10).

The Pulitzer Prize-winning poet Annie Dillard wrote that some of the Christian mystics spoke of a created substance, called Holy the Firm, that underlies all other created reality and that itself touches the Absolute. Those who tinker with matter and space and formulate ideas have no *idea* as real as the reality that ties us all to the Absolute.

What can any artist set on fire but his world? What can any people bring to the altar but all it has ever owned in the thin towns or over the desolate plains? What can an artist use but materials, such as they are? ... His face is flame like a seraph's, lighting the kingdom of God for the people to see; his life goes up in the works; his feet are waxen and salt. He is holy and he is firm, spanning all the long gap with the length of his love, in flawed imitation of Christ on the cross stretched both ways unbroken and thorned. So must the work be also, in touch with, in touch with, in touch with; spanning the gap, from here to eternity, home.

These are but intimations that the self can experience reality at a deeper and more profound level of feeling than our five senses can register. To dismiss these feelings is to deny the existence of the self. To hurt these feelings is to wound the self beyond repair by ordinary means. To violate the integrity of a person's feelings, especially those of a child, is to injure the core of the self and produce feelings of outrage and pain. To abuse the spirit of another is to bruise the feeling self so that it cannot feel, and that part of the self disappears into the unconscious as though dead.

"Don't mind Ray—he's just got his feelings hurt!" Even now I want to cry out, "Please! Mind Ray, for when his feelings hurt no one feels as bad as he does."

Renewing and Repairing Our Feelings

A particular brand of unhappiness, when carried into adulthood, lies beneath the surface of everyday life. Like a virus that clings secretly to a strand of tissue, it erupts into searing pain under stress and strain. If we succeed in neutralizing it for a time, and even believe that it has disappeared forever, it reappears as if on cue to make us feel unwanted, unneeded, unloved and absolutely sure that no one feels as bad as we do. It may be triggered by a sharp exchange of words, a cutting reminder that we failed to perform a task. Or it may seep into our soul like an evening fog when we are most vulnerable. The psychologists call it depression, but we know it as despair. It is, I believe, a childhood affliction called hurt feelings.

Some days we dare to believe that we are really a princess turned into a frog by a wicked witch and that if only some prince came along to kiss us we would be transformed. That wish turns into mockery when the sinking feeling comes that we were only a frog to begin with. And there are no kisses that can turn a real frog into a princess. This is what despair does to fairy tales.

No magic potions exist that can make us feel better when our feelings have been injured and driven into a dark cellar of the soul. Feelings cannot be forgotten like names and places, though they can be repressed. Feelings do not disappear into the labyrinth of the brain circuits like other pieces of data, lost forever. Feelings are the self, its own way of existing, and when feelings are hurt the self is in trauma.

Few of us have been hurt so deeply that we have not found a place of renewal and repair through the ordinary experiences of growth and life. Most of us, however, carry within us feelings that have never been comforted; most of us have spots on our soul on which no light shines. To discover the way to renew hurt feelings, we need to see how deep these hurt feelings have gone and how hard it is to open them up to healing. The stories of others can often help us to discover the way ourselves.

The one person in the Bible who is so compelling in this regard is Judas, the disciple who betrayed Jesus and, in the depth of despair and remorse, hung himself. In *The Gospel According to Judas* I imagined a conversation between the resurrected Jesus and Judas after he killed himself. Judas does not quickly respond to the living and loving presence of Jesus.

I am confused. You tell me that I am an answer to prayer and that you have prayed for me to be healed. But I sealed my fate with my fatal act of betrayal. Death was the final act of mercy that delivered my soul from the torment of life. I feel nothing, neither love nor hope.

How is it, Judas, that you feel such anger at me if you have killed all feeling?

Because you bring back to me all that I died to get away from. I closed the door to my life and sealed it with my own death. But now you have opened that door again. You have awakened all of the old feelings, but none that are new.

God is not the God of the dead, Judas, but of the living. Because I live, you also shall live.

Yes, I remember that you taught us that. But that had reference to Abraham, Isaac and Jacob, who all died in faith. They may each have had many failures, but none of them failed as I did. My failure was fatal. I killed faith and tore the star of hope out of the black night, leaving only a gaping wound that will never heal.

And I have come to you through that tear in the fabric of despair to touch your life again with healing grace and divine love.

But surely there are limits, even to God's grace. And I, of all persons, have passed beyond that limit. My name shall be remembered without pity and my act of betrayal my epitaph. No one weeps for me.

History has not been kind to Judas. He had no one to blame but himself, we are told. He was not the victim of abuse. He was the betrayer, not the betrayed. Others were sure to condemn him, but he did not wait for their verdict. Judas heaps on himself scorn without pity and judgment without mercy. The effect is the same as if he had been accused and rejected by others.

What we don't realize is that injury to the feeling self is of serious consequence regardless of the source. When we seek our healing by trying to reach out to the source of our injury rather than to our damaged self, we are taking the long way home. But how can we approach our own hurt feelings without a relationship? And where is the relationship that will hear our complaint, tolerate our accusations and yet provide a source of healing?

As Jesus hung on the cross, he had every reason to blame his humiliating nakedness on his abandonment by his disciples and certainly on Judas, his betrayer. But it was not to them he turned in his distress, but to God. "My God, my God, why have you forsaken me?" he cried (Matthew 27:46). "Why have *you* forsaken me, God?" Let the emphasis be made boldly. Jesus could have blamed the devil and lashed out at his enemies. Instinctively, though, he turned to what we might call the worst-case scenario. Why wouldn't his Father in heaven, who once had called him "my beloved Son" (Matthew 3:17), intervene and prevent this abuse? Dare he charge the very name of divine love with turning away from him in his great hour of need? Yes, he would and he must. For we do not reach the core of our injured self until we demand of God an accounting for our soul's condition.

Between our souls and God there are no intermediaries, neither angels nor demons. Our very existence is grounded in the self-existence of God. If we strike out at him, we are in his presence, and only in his presence can we feel the stroke of his love and hear again his spoken word—"my beloved child." When we are bruised at the core of our deepest self, there is no one left against whom we can raise our voice, except God.

To realize that this is what we have done is terrifying. Yet we discover to our amazement that we have made contact with the One who has the power to absorb our pain and return it as love. God receives our curses and returns them as blessings.

The prophets of old knew this truth well, and in their suffering they lifted their lament to God in a litany of accusation and hope. Consider Job, for example:

And now my soul is poured out within me;
    days of affliction have taken hold of me.

The night racks my bones,
      and the pain that gnaws me takes no rest.
With violence he seizes my garment;
      he grasps me by the collar of my tunic.
He has cast me into the mire,
      and I have become like dust and ashes.
I cry to you and you do not answer me;
      I stand, and you merely look at me.
You have turned cruel to me;
      with the might of your hand you persecute me. (Job 30:16-21)

Job finally received from God both his answer and a blessing that was greater than the blessing of his former days (Job 42:12).

With a series of complaints the prophet Jeremiah similarly charged God with devastating his life:

I am one who has seen affliction
      under the rod of God's wrath;
he has driven and brought me
      into darkness without any light. . . .
He has walled me about so that I cannot escape;
      he has put heavy chains on me;
though I call and cry for help,
      he shuts out my prayer;
he has blocked my ways with hewn stones,
      he has made my paths crooked. . . .
He has made my teeth grind on gravel,
      and made me cower in ashes;
my soul is bereft of peace;
      I have forgotten what happiness is;
so I say, "Gone is my glory,
      and all that I had hoped for from the LORD." . . .
But this I call to mind,
      and therefore I have hope:

The steadfast love of the LORD never ceases,
    his mercies never come to an end;
they are new every morning;
    great is your faithfulness. (Lamentations 3:1-2, 7-9, 16-18, 21-24)

As we read this today, we are shocked at such language accusing God of deliberately causing terrible distress. We have been taught to express love and adoration to God, not anger and accusation. But this only reveals how far we have removed God from our deepest feelings. There can be no other point of beginning for the repair and renewing of our feelings than to direct them to God. Whatever our concept of God, we must discover the reality of God at the depth of our feelings.

God Feels Hurt Feelings

God feels hurt feelings, and he feels them most accurately when they are undiluted and outrageous. "When you search for me, you will find me; if you seek me with all your heart, I will let you find me, says the LORD" (Jeremiah 29:13). "All your heart" does not mean that you have succeeded in assembling all of the pieces or have integrated all parts into the whole. "All" is a degree of depth, not of breadth. The one part of the heart that is unerring in its quest is the part that hurts the most. When our feelings are hurt so deeply, *all* we can do is to cry out to the One who is the source of our existence.

We must be careful, then, not to silence those who cry out in their pain. To dismiss the plight of others as due to self-pity or even self-inflicted injury is itself a betrayal of the bond we share with all who suffer abuse and violence to the spirit. Only when we understand the effect of abuse on the deepest feelings of the self will we understand, in some measure, the way to renewal and repair of our own feelings. The unhappiness of hurt feelings is a continuum on which all of us have a place. From those who have received the less injury to those who have suffered the greatest abuse, there stretches a cord of familiar feeling. We learn from each other and listen to each other's stories of recovery in order to find clues to our own healing.

Laura is a grown woman, married and with children of her own. She sought professional therapy when she could no longer cope with feelings of being a failure as a wife and mother. She had withdrawn to the point of causing concern among her family members and friends. After months of talking about her feelings with the therapist, she still could not get past a block in her memory of childhood years. It was as though she did not exist prior to her twelfth birthday, for she had no feelings or memories of those years.

As part of her therapy she created drawings in an attempt to express feelings that could not be consciously remembered. A pattern begin to emerge. In most of the drawings she drew a daisy with a dark spot at the center. One day, reviewing these drawings with the therapist, she noticed that in the center of one daisy she had drawn a small face instead of a black dot. As she reflected on what this might mean, a sudden rush of feelings overpowered her, and she remembered the daisy wallpaper in her childhood bedroom. Through this opening in her blocked feelings, she remembered being sexually abused by her father in that bedroom and how she had distanced herself from her body during those incidents by imagining herself hiding in the daisies.

The pain of recalling and reexperiencing those feelings was almost more than Laura could bear. Through the weeks of therapy that followed, however, she began the work of repairing her feelings and regaining her capacity to have positive feelings of self-worth. She will always have knowledge of the incidents of abuse, but her feelings about these incidents are now owned as her feelings as a grown woman, not as an injured child. Now that she has integrated the incident of abuse into her life story, her feelings are those of an adult who has brought those feelings into the orbit of her total feelings about herself. Because she now has *good* feelings about herself, she can experience and express more accurate feelings about the bad things in her life.

Steps to Recovery

1. When it hurts, say so. The first step in the repair of damage to the self when feelings are hurt is to accept freedom to express the outrage and anger that has accumulated. These feelings are unerring in their power to rediscover the self that has been driven into hiding or splintered into fragments. The feeling of injustice at the violation of our very being is a sign of the integration of the self with what is most authentic—its right to exist and to be loved.

2. Take your hurt feelings directly to God. The next step is to press the accusation and lay the charge against someone ultimately responsible for our well-being. At first our blame is directed toward the one who has injured or abused us. Or we may move beyond the realm of the natural and accuse the devil or his demons of afflicting us. Thus they said of Judas, "Satan entered into him" (John 13:27). He may well have thought this of himself, but there was no power of healing in turning to demons as the cause, as if to remove them would restore him to Jesus. This kind of blaming may be part of the first step. But when we realize that our grievance is greater than the indictment of the abuser nearest to hand, we have moved beyond the first stage of repairing the self.

A significant aspect of the religion of the Hebrew people in the Old Testament and the continuing tradition through Jesus Christ was that in the encounter with Yahweh (the God of covenant) and Jesus (the incarnate Son of God), people were freed from the supposed power of both local deities and local demons. The God who confronts the people permits them to have "no other gods" and allows them no other source of both weal and woe but himself. Through his prophet Isaiah, the Lord says, "I form light and create darkness, I make weal and create woe; I the LORD do all these things" (Isaiah 45:7). While this sounds strange to our ears, it is quite liberating to be able to be free from the "strange gods" and "familiar spirits" that torment us.

When we split God off from his responsibility for evil in the cosmos, we have given as much power to the devil as to God. At the same time, we suffer the split within ourselves, with part of us becoming the evil and part the good. While we confess that God is the greater power of good in the abstract, the pervasive and destructive power of evil in actuality can make us practical atheists.

In allowing us (like Job and Jeremiah) to charge him with the evil that has fallen upon us, God does not want us to think that he is the author of evil. The Bible teaches us that God's power is greater than the power of evil and that Jesus has overcome Satan's power to inflict evil on us (Hebrews 2:14-15). God, as a good parent, does take responsibility, and we can trust him as the source of our healing and hope. In going to God we find the answer to our most profound questions about suffering and the presence of evil in the world. But we go to God with our feelings, even of outrage, in order to find the sole power of the good.

In his play *The Boy with a Cart* Christopher Fry presents us with a parable of faith. Cuthman, a shepherd boy, believes that God helps him guard his sheep from straying. He draws a circle with his shepherd's crook around them, asking God to keep them within the invisible boundary—and God does. When informed by the people of the village that his father has suddenly died, Cuthman is stricken with the thought that he has "stolen God" away from his father to guard his sheep. The "people of England," like a chorus, chant their challenge to him:

How is your faith now, Cuthman?
Your faith that the warm world hatched,
That spread its unaccustomed colour
Up on the rock, game and detached?

You see how sorrow rises, Cuthman,
How sorrow rises like the heat
Even up to the plumed hills
and the quickest feet.

Pain is low against the ground
And grows like a weed.
Is God still in the air
And in the seed?
Is God still in the air
Now that the sun is down?
They are afraid in the city,
Sleepless in the town,
Cold on the roads
Desperate by the river.
Can faith for long elude
Prevailing fever?

The people of Israel knew that their God was ultimately responsible for all that happened to them. Despite the so-called powers that might threaten them from above or below, they looked to God for deliverance. The apostle Paul expresses in his eloquent doxology the same assurance: "Who will separate us from the love of Christ? . . . For I am convinced that neither death, nor life, nor angels, nor rulers, nor things present, nor things to come, nor powers, nor height, nor depth, nor anything else in all creation, will be able to separate us from the love of God in Christ Jesus our Lord" (Romans 8:35, 38-39). We can be assured that no evil lies outside of God's loving power; he *can* repair and restore our lives. The basis for all true healing and growth rests in this truth.

Those who become our caregivers when we are children become our "local deities." We endow them with virtual supernatural power to care for our needs and to control our destiny. Later, we include in our panel of deities the priests and sometimes the therapists. Some of them become quite demonic, in actuality, damaging us through carelessness and sometimes outright cruelty. The terrible torment of having our feelings hurt and our selves damaged so severely is that the offense comes from those whom we trusted to care for us.

It is the destruction of this trust that becomes the greatest loss in being abused by those whom we thought loved us. This is why the second step in the repairing of the self is the freedom to approach God, who is ultimately responsible, and—in prayer and forthright conversation—present our case.

3. Trust the ones who listen and love. The third step in recovery is the actual restoring of the capacity to trust. The loss of the feeling of trust is the most serious of all losses to the self. Trusting ourselves is directly linked with our capacity to trust others. When we do not trust our own feelings, we do not trust the feelings of others, and therefore we do not trust their words or actions.

Ted Turner, named by *Time* magazine as Man of the Year in its January 6, 1992, issue, is said to have been a practicing Christian who had planned to be a missionary. When he was twenty years old, his seventeen-year-old sister Mary Jane died of a distressing and disfiguring disease. "The loss of his sister killed his faith in God," the magazine reported. Faith in God requires trust; when that trust is destroyed, it demolishes faith as well. Perhaps young Turner was denied the expression of his anger at God by some "local deity"; perhaps his anger was deemed inappropriate. In any event, he doesn't seem to have entered into serious wrestling with God over the tragedy.

With step one we discover the freedom to express outrage and anger when we have been violated and injured. Then, in the second step, we press our case directly to God, who is ultimately responsible, not fearing his rejection or disapproval.

If we have taken these steps, we will have discovered that we can, finally, trust our feelings of outrage and injustice as being accurate and legitimate (step three). Some integration of our self with our feelings has been achieved. If we have been given permission to address our grievance to the One who has ultimate responsibility—in this case, the God of the universe—and we have not been struck down for this presumption, we may conclude that our feelings have been vindicated.

Hurt Feelings Can Be Repaired

Repairing of the damage done to the self through injury and abuse involves risking the self again to the hazards of love and faith. This is not a performance, a task demanded of us so we can qualify once more for a religious marathon. Rather, we hear the voice of Jesus encouraging us to become like a child again and so enter the kingdom of God (Matthew 18:2-3). We remember that for a child the relation with the parent without any intermediary is the continuum on which identity is formed. When the child feels most fragmented and has internalized negative feelings about him- or herself, he or she will often express these to the parent as "I hate you!" The wise parent will accept these feelings as authentic and will communicate acceptance even with those feelings. Feelings, as I have said, are not extraneous to the self but *are* the self.

The child actually repairs the relationship with the parent through expressing these feelings, even of hatred. The parent repairs the relationship with the child by integrating these feelings (and thus the self of the child) into the relationship. When the parent takes the negative feelings, the child is freed to recover positive feelings about himself or herself and can later acknowledge that the expression of anger and hatred was inappropriate.

Trust is repaired only when the feelings most authentic to the self have been expressed and validated and we receive the affirmation that we are under the power of blessing rather than cursing. The apostle Paul, a trustworthy guide in these matters due to his own process of repairing the damage done through his failure to rightly perceive Jesus at first, encourages us: "The faith that you have, have as your own conviction before God. Blessed are those who have no reason to condemn themselves because of what they approve" (Romans 14:22). The apostle John kindly reminds us, "And by this we will know that we are from the truth and will reassure our hearts before him whenever our hearts condemn us; for God is greater than our hearts, and he knows everything" (1 John 3:19-20).

The popular psychology of our day encourages us to "get in touch with our feelings" or to "discover the child within us." I have tried to show that feelings are not something that flows through a faucet, waiting to be turned on. Rather, feelings *are* the self and are crucial to its development from child into adult. When hurt feelings are carried along as the self's core identity, we do not have a happy child that has become lost but an injured child that needs to be healed and grown up.

Happiness is more than a child's momentary delight. As I said earlier, true happiness arises from the developed feeling of joy and expectation of the future. We discover happiness when the promise of our childhood develops into the productivity of our maturity. Paul discovered that the child's feelings could grow into maturity when he wrote, "When I was a child, I spoke like a child, I thought like a child, I reasoned like a child; when I became an adult, I put an end to childish ways" (1 Corinthians 13:11).

Everything that makes me a happy child I learned when I grew up Let's go on to experience that adventure.

Part 2

Everything That Makes Me Happy I Learned When I Grew Up

5

I Learned
to Find My
Own Boundaries

*S*omething there is that doesn't love a wall, that wants it down," opined Robert Frost. His neighbor, however, had his own philosophy: "Good fences make good neighbors." Frost preferred open space between people, permitting them to mingle by choice while respecting each other's personal space. He thus implied that even where there are no fences, there need to be boundaries that define the social intercourse and personal identity of every person. He seemed to suggest that where boundaries are respected there will be no need for fences. "Before I built a wall," reasoned Frost, "I'd ask to know what I was walling in or walling out."

One mark of people who have found happiness is that they find their own boundaries in life acceptable. To be acceptable a boundary need not be one that we draw for ourselves, but it must allow us to grow and expand into the full dimension of ourselves. The boundaries that define our lives need not be rigid, but they must be real. Boundaries are the emotional constructs that protect, enhance and sometimes restrict our integrity as individuals.

Our boundaries are meant to expand and contract with changing circumstances, relationships and opportunities. They are to be like the living tissue of our lungs, filling with the intoxicating freedom of our dreams at one moment and expressing the warm breath of gratitude for our duty in the next.

The Boundaries of Birth

Some boundaries are determined for us at birth. We do not choose our own parents, nor did our parents choose our gender and physical configuration. For some, conception and birth came about through planning and prayer; for others they came by carelessness and compulsive passion. No matter! In either case we wake up to discover that much has already been chosen for us by love or lot. "We are born into other people's intentions," wrote Theodore Roszak. "We learn our names and our natures at their hands, and they cannot teach us more truth than they know or will freely tell."

Our first birth sets the boundary of our existence from which we can only go forward. The "birthmarks" of this boundary are only discovered later and, like coordinates on a map, locate us in particular time and space with indelible ink. Few of us change the name given to us at birth, even if we would have preferred another one. Gender identity is relatively fixed at birth for the majority, as well as the racial, ethnic and physiological features that define us. Whether we "choose" to accept these boundaries within which we live our life is another matter. But we cannot choose until choice is born within us.

There is a second birth of the self, then, the birth of self-awareness. In a sense this is the real birth of the self. It is not instantaneous, like our conception, but occurs gradually and imperceptibly until it emerges, like the man from whom Jesus cast out the demons, "clothed and in [its] right mind" (Luke 8:35).

In *An American Childhood* Annie Dillard wrote of her own awakening to self-consciousness:

> Children ten years old wake up and find themselves here, discover themselves to have been here all along; is this sad? They wake like sleepwalkers, in full stride; they wake like people brought back from cardiac arrest or from drowning: *in medias res,* surrounded by familiar people and objects, equipped with a hundred skills. They know the neighborhood, they can read and write English, they are old hands at the commonplace mysteries, and yet they feel themselves to have just stepped off the boat, just converged with their bodies, just flown down from a trance, to lodge in an eerily familiar life already well under way.
>
> I woke in bits, like all children, piecemeal over the years. I discovered myself and the world, and forgot them, and discovered them again. I woke at intervals until, by that September when Father went down the river, the intervals of waking tipped the scales, and I was more often awake than not. I noticed this process of waking, and predicted with terrifying logic that one of these years not far away I would be awake continuously and never slip back, and never be free of myself again.

We become aware of our selves long after the emotional map that defines our feelings and controls our behavior is firmly in place. The terrain of our feeling self may be marked by rigid and restrictive boundaries caused by trauma to the self in early emotional experiences. Feelings of panic when left alone, fear when threatened by the unknown, anger when abused by hurting words or physical pain—these feelings can cause the self to set up walls that harden and become opaque as stone, binding and limiting our existence. When the self reaches conscious awareness of itself, these boundaries seem "normal" and essential, despite the limits they set on our life.

Others may have had early childhood experiences in which boundaries were never clearly formed and the self became enmeshed with others. This can lead to a lack of self-identity and a failure of the self to mark out the boundaries between self and others. For the boundary of the self to be merged with the boundary of others can be as destructive and defeating as the overly rigid boundaries that isolate the self from others.

The boundaries that are acquired as we grow and experience relationship with others can be clarified and changed. We become more aware of the influence of the past on our feeling self and become more open to growth of the self with newly discovered choices. In the comic strip *Peanuts,* Linus says to Charlie Brown, "I think we should stop worrying about tomorrow and expect more from today." "That's giving up," Charlie Brown responds. "I'm still hoping yesterday will get better." For many people, today cannot be good until yesterday gets better.

Dennis and Lucy Guernsey, in *Birthmarks,* speak of "psychological birthmarks" as "imprints" from our family history experienced as toxic emotional deposits that distort and hinder our growth and development. Nevertheless, they suggest, "the past only influences the present; it doesn't determine it." We are not bound to everything we have experienced. The key is realizing that we can change negative experiences of the past.

But the empowerment to transform our emotional relation to the boundaries of our life does not come from psychological awareness alone. This transforming power can be likened to a third "birth"—a birth of spiritual awareness.

The Transforming Birth of Spiritual Awareness

He was born in Tarsus, a city in the province of Asia Minor, and named after the first king of Israel, Saul. By his own admission, he was born into a privileged and highly prized status. He was a Jew, a male and a free-born citizen of Rome (Acts 22:28). As such, he thought, he had the best of both worlds. Circumcised in accordance with the Jewish law, he was raised to become a member of the most prestigious religious sect of his day, the Pharisees. With fanatical zeal he hunted down Christians and delivered them over to persecution and death (Acts 22:4, 26:10; Philippians 3:6). That he later became the apostle Paul, one of the most dynamic and effective Christian leaders of the first century, is a story that reveals the transforming power of spiritual birth.

Near the end of his life, writing from a Roman prison, he was to say of himself, "I have learned to be content with whatever I have. I know what it is to have little, and I know what it is to have plenty. In any and all circumstances I have learned the secret of being well-fed and of going hungry, of having plenty and of being in need. I can do all things through him who strengthens me" (Philippians 4:11-13). Paul has discovered the secret to happiness that enabled King David to pen these lines:

The LORD is my chosen portion and my cup;
    you hold my lot.
The boundary lines have fallen for me in pleasant places;
    I have a goodly heritage. (Psalm 16:5-6)

David recalls the days when Joshua led the people of Israel out of the forty years of wandering in the desert into the Promised Land. When the conquest of the Promised Land was completed, the leaders of the twelve tribes assembled for the boundary lines to be chosen that would give each tribe their own land. Each tribe received its inheritance through the random casting of lots (Joshua 14).

These divisions became the "birth boundaries" of the people of Israel. Not every parcel was of equal value. Some of the land was fertile, while other portions were barren and steep. Not everyone received his heart's desire. But David envisioned each one accepting the boundary lines that defined his share in the promise as having "fallen in pleasant places." This acceptance of one's lot in life became a metaphor for David as he reflected on the events that framed the landscape of his life. Tears as well as triumphs were part of the mosaic, with both highlights and shadows cast by the soft light of God's benediction on his life.

How, we may ask, is it possible to come to terms with the boundaries in our life with such positive feelings? And is it fair to think we should? Can the smoldering fire of resentment against the arbitrary and sometimes unfair boundaries that hedge in our life be extinguished so easily?

"Well and good for you to feel that way, King David and Paul the apostle," we want to cry out. "Easy for you to say. But saying it doesn't make it happen for me!" Doesn't the psalm of praise turn sour and become a pious platitude when sung to the suffering soul? Solomon was more realistic when he said, "Like vinegar on a wound is one who sings songs to a heavy heart" (Proverbs 25:20).

Note the fascinating contrast between King Saul and David, his successor. Saul was chosen by the people as their king because of his superior physical appearance and military prowess (1 Samuel 9:2). As it turned out, he rebelled against the boundary set for him by God and, through his disobedience, ended his days as a vindictive and bitter man, taking his own life rather than suffer the indignity of defeat in battle (1 Samuel 15:1-35; 31:1-7). David, on the other hand, was chosen by God while still a shepherd boy. While incurring God's disfavor at times, he kept his heart where God's gracious love could shine on him. King Saul was soothed by David's songs but never learned their meaning. David gained the kingdom but did not forfeit the contentment of a shepherd's heart. King Saul fought against the boundaries in his life, while King David found his own boundaries to be the gracious stroke of God's love, defining his place and giving him peace.

From this we might conclude that some of us are born like Saul and some like David. "Can Ethiopians change their skin or leopards their spots?" asked Jeremiah, when confronted with the hardness of heart of his contemporaries (Jeremiah 13:23). There is ample evidence that once the personality is formed it is very difficult to effect a transformation. We are all witnesses to the fact that people around us don't easily change their attitudes and actions. Some of us have tried to bring change in our lives with little lasting success. Behavior modification techniques used by psychologists may succeed in modifying our actions, but rarely do they allow us to transform anger into gentleness and unhappiness into happiness.

With Saul of Tarsus, however, we have quite a different story. Here is a man whose birth boundaries were more like those of his namesake, King Saul, than like those of David. Yet his is a story of a transformation so dramatic and deep that we are compelled to listen and learn. The transforming birth of spiritual awareness for Saul reached back into his yesterdays and reoriented his relation to his birth boundaries. At the same time it opened up new horizons for self-fulfillment and new dimensions of self-awareness. When Saul, the raging zealot of religious righteousness, becomes Paul, the apostle of love, we have an answer to Jeremiah's question: "Yes, some leopards do change their spots!"

The dramatic conversion of Saul of Tarsus on the road to Damascus is well documented in the New Testament. Luke records the incident in the ninth chapter of Acts. Paul himself recounts the story in some detail at least twice as part of his defense when arrested as a ringleader of the "sect" called Nazarenes and charged with creating civil unrest (Acts 22; 26). The focal point of the story is the encounter with the risen Jesus Christ, who appeared to Saul when he was seeking out Christians to bring them bound back to Jerusalem. Blinded by the laser light of Jesus' presence, he was led to Damascus, where Ananias laid hands on him and prayed for him. As a result he received his sight and was filled with the Holy Spirit. He was baptized and immediately began to proclaim in the synagogues that Jesus was the Son of God and the promised Messiah (Acts 9).

Isn't there a shared subconscious longing for such a drama to change our lives in an immediate and transforming moment? While we are amazed and transfixed by the stunning event of Saul's conversion, we think back to our own struggles to subdue contrary passions and feel more alone than ever. Spiritual awareness, we hazard a guess, does not erase the old emotions and paste in new ones as easily as hitting a few keystrokes on the computer keyboard.

Let's look at the process of this transformation. How does such a birth of spiritual awareness and emotional change occur? Saul's concept of Jesus Christ was changed instantly when he encountered him as the risen Lord. Formerly he had seen Jesus as an impostor and blasphemer for daring to call God his Father. Now Saul acknowledged him to be the Messiah and Lord of his life. Did this dramatic religious conversion produce an immediate personal transformation? We shall see.

Saul, who later changed his name to Paul, attributes the transforming of his life to the "new sight" that began directly as a result of this encounter and continued through the rest of his life. The gospel of Christ, as Paul later called it, was not of human origin, nor was he taught it by others, but "I received it through a revelation of Jesus Christ" (Galatians 1:12). The "wisdom of God" that was revealed through Jesus Christ, as Paul spoke of it, does not come through our natural understanding but through the Spirit of God. Quoting the prophet Isaiah, Paul wrote, " 'What no eye has seen, nor ear heard, nor the human heart conceived, what God has prepared for those who love him'—these things God has revealed to us through the Spirit" (1 Corinthians 2:9-10). Following his conversion Paul isolated himself from others during an extended stay in Arabia and then returned to Damascus. He went to Jerusalem three years later to meet the other apostles after that period of reflection and ministry (Galatians 1:15-20).

So far we have seen the amazing paradigm shift that occurred for Paul in his concept of Jesus Christ and his knowledge of God through the wisdom of the Spirit. His "boundary shift," however, did not occur so easily, particularly in regard to those inner boundaries that have to do with feelings, attitudes and actions. Follow me as we retrace the stages of his transformation from Saul the fearful Pharisee to Paul the beloved brother through the painful process of inner boundary shifts.

The Inward Journey to the Peaceable Life

I suggested earlier that Saul's birth boundaries were religious and rigid. He was born a Jewish male, was schooled at the highest level of Judaism under the scholar Gamaliel (Acts 22:3), and was a high-ranking member of the scrupulous Pharisee sect. By his own admission he had "advanced in Judaism beyond many among my people of the same age" and was "far more zealous for the traditions of my ancestors" (Galatians 1:14).

This fanatical zeal arrests our attention. Luke tells us that Saul heard the witness of a dying Stephen, stoned to death for his faith, and "approved of their killing him." While the Christians were still grieving over Stephen's death, Luke says Saul was "ravaging the church by entering house after house; dragging off both men and women, he committed them to prison" (Acts 8:1-3). As Luke begins the account of Saul's conversion he writes, "Meanwhile, Saul, still breathing threats and murder against the disciples of the Lord . . ." (Acts 9:1).

While Saul intellectually exceeded his peers in Judaism, he also surpassed them in his rage and fury against the Christians. There was much of the same "evil spirit" in Saul of Tarsus as there was in King Saul, as he sought to find and kill David. Saul's hatred of Christians exceeded the bounds of simple disbelief that Jesus was the Messiah. His outraged actions betray an inner turmoil that was boiling over, seeking live targets on which to expend his deadly and almost demonic hatred.

What accounts for this fury and fanaticism in one so devoutly religious? As Paul recounts the story of his conversion before King Agrippa, he tells us that Jesus spoke to him in Hebrew, saying, "Saul, Saul, why are you persecuting me? It hurts you to kick against the goads" (Acts 26:14). "Kick against the goads" is an interesting phrase. A goad is a sharp stick used to prod animals in order to make them follow your commands. The animal becomes enraged and kicks back against the goad, making the pain even more severe and setting off a vicious cycle of goading and kicking.

This provides a clue for us that what inflamed Saul's fury was not the intellectual issue of whether Jesus was the Jewish Messiah but a "fire in his belly," to use a current phrase in pop psychology. The Christians who served as the targets for Saul's hatred were actually the goad of Christ, prodding Saul, crouched as he was behind his birth boundaries. The goad did not cause the anger but only prodded it into action. Smoldering within Saul there was a bank of red-hot coals, waiting to erupt in fury and rage against any threat to his personal boundary of legal righteousness obtained by observance of the Jewish law.

The early Christians were terrified of Saul. Even Ananias, who was instructed in a vision from the Lord to go and pray for Saul after he was blinded, protested, "Lord, I have heard from many about this man, how much evil he has done to your saints in Jerusalem" (Acts 9:13). When Saul did arrive in Jerusalem, even after three years of ministry in Damascus, Luke tells us that "he attempted to join the disciples; and they were all afraid of him, for they did not believe that he was a disciple" (Acts 9:26). Barnabas (whose name means "son of consolation") interceded for him, assuring the other disciples that he indeed had been converted and could be trusted. Barnabas apparently sensed in Saul the truth of his spiritual rebirth.

Saul deserved his reputation: he *had* been a ruthless and vicious enemy of the Christians. The early disciples were not convinced that a man driven by such emotional fury could change so quickly into someone whom they could trust. As it turned out, the change from Saul to Paul was more than an instant change of name. It took place over time, with some painful incidents suffered by both Paul and his friends.

Barnabas, the very one who had interceded for Paul at Jerusalem, felt the fury of Paul's anger at a later point. Following the first missionary journey on which Paul and Barnabas acted as a team, Paul determined that they should retrace their earlier route and encourage the new churches (Acts 15:36). Barnabas was agreeable but wanted to take along John Mark, who had abandoned them during the first mission. Paul was furious. Luke recalls the incident: "The disagreement became so sharp that they parted company; Barnabas took Mark with him and sailed away to Cyprus. But Paul chose Silas and set out" (Acts 15:39-40).

The English translation weakens the strong word that Luke used to record the conflict. Luke used the Greek word *paroxysmos* to describe Paul's reaction to Barnabas; this word suggests such a violent display of anger and temper that one virtually is out of control. The fact that loyal Barnabas could become the target of Paul's outburst and that a separation occurred over this incident reveals to us how Paul had to struggle with still-unresolved feelings and emotions despite his conversion.

Paul became famous for the great hymn of love inserted into his letter to the factious and fighting Corinthians (1 Corinthians 13): "Love is patient; love is kind; love is not envious or boastful or arrogant or rude. It does not insist on its own way; it is not irritable or resentful." The English word *irritable* translates into the Greek *paroxysmos,* the very word that Luke uses to describe Paul's outburst against Barnabas (Acts 15:39). Love does not engage in paroxysms of anger, Paul was later to write. How marvelous that Paul used the same word Luke had chosen to describe his outrageous behavior as a contrast to the restraint and respect demonstrated by love.

While Paul had a dramatic conversion experience that turned his life around, the inner transformation took place more slowly. The short fuse on his anger gave vent to deeper feelings still unknown and untried. It was to reach these deeper feelings that the Spirit of God came into his life—not to deny the feelings but to release them from his birth boundaries and attach them to new horizons of self-awareness and self-fulfillment.

Paul still had passion burning in his bones, but it no longer was an uncontrollable fire. He had received the "stroke of love" from Christ and became open to the transforming power of that spiritual rebirth. God's love moved behind the boundaries of Saul of Tarsus and, patiently and persuasively, empowered him to move toward a new horizon of self-awareness. With these new horizons came, for the first time, the power to choose the boundaries that were his by birth and to change the boundaries that were his by default.

Those of us who work with computers know that one of the first things we must learn is how to change the default settings programmed into the software. These default settings mean that we don't have to program the computer each time it is booted up. The software allows for changes to be made in basic settings during operation, such as typeface, page format and printer specifications. But unless we make changes in the default settings, when the computer is turned off these temporary changes are lost, and the next time we boot up the software the original default settings remain.

Some of the birth boundaries that control our behavior and program our happiness are like default settings in the computer software. Our feelings, by default, operate in an emotional mode originally programmed by the self through early experiences. Anger, fearful loss of self and a sense of hopelessness are examples of such emotional settings that determine our reactions, by default, each time we "turn on to life." When the love of God continues to shine on us and the Spirit of God searches out the depth of our feeling self to heal us, these default settings of the emotional life can be reprogrammed.

Here is our clue to the process of transformation. It is not our boundaries that need to be shifted in order to fulfill our desires. The horizon of self-awareness needs to be expanded in order for us to fulfill our desire *within* our boundaries. Finding these new horizons is the key to contentment and self-acceptance.

The Outward Journey to the Fulfilled Life
Susie taught me a lesson that I will never forget. Afflicted with cerebral palsy since birth, she cannot dress or feed herself. She talks with

difficulty, in words as twisted and tortured as the spastic motions required to force them out. But with an unusual passion for life Susie completed college and a master's degree in theology, taking several courses that I had taught. When she received her degree, I asked her what she intended to do. Perceiving her within the boundaries I had set for her, I suggested, "Perhaps you will have a significant ministry to others who suffer handicaps in life."

"No," she said, "most of them haven't forgiven God for who they are, and I have."

Susie was experiencing horizons that had expanded far beyond her birth boundaries. Forgiving God for who she was—indeed! Whom should she hold responsible for the constricting birth boundaries that imprisoned her free and joyous spirit within a body she could not control? She expanded the horizon of her complaint, like Job of old, and laid the offense at the throne of God. When the Lord who created her did not dodge or duck, she concluded that the only freeing thing left was to forgive. Having lodged the charge against God with all of the emotional power at her disposal, she discovered that she also had the power to forgive him.

Susie had no sense that God had caused her birth deformity, nor did she feel that he had willed this condition for some inscrutable purpose of his own. Her dealings with God were not theological but deeply existential. She sought to touch with her feelings the face of God and trace out the profile of One who could allow her to question the fairness of being born with a disability and yet not deflect the question back on her. In a sense she felt that God had taken responsibility for what happened to her, even though he had not willingly inflicted this on her.

In holding God responsible but not blaming him, she found an ally in her predicament. Releasing God from blame became possible when God assumed responsibility. Her life now had two sides to it. The one side of her life was restricting and confining. The other side was open and freeing. This is what she meant by forgiving God for who she was.

She experienced God as a forgiving and merciful God, and this empowered her to release God from blame for her disability. In bringing to God her complaint, she experienced the transforming power of God's grace.

The power of forgiveness toward another human being is not an inward journey but an outward journey. To free another person from an offense against one's own life is to free oneself, to discover a power that expands the horizons of self-awareness beyond all the given boundaries and burdens. Jesus gave the key: "Whatever you loose on earth will be loosed in heaven" (Matthew 16:19). To discover the inner resources to forgive God of an offense against one's life is to experience a spiritual power and freedom no birth boundary can contain.

From Saul, who became Paul, I learned the transforming power of God's forgiveness and what it means to say, "I have learned to be content with whatever I have. I know what it is to have little, and I know what it is to have plenty. In any and all circumstances I have learned the secret of being well-fed and of going hungry, of having plenty and of being in need. I can do all things through him who strengthens me" (Philippians 4:11-13).

From Susie, my spiritual mentor in discovering new horizons, I learned what it means to go beyond contentment and to say with King David:

The LORD is my chosen portion and my cup;
   you hold my lot.
The boundary lines have fallen for me in pleasant places;
   I have a goodly heritage. (Psalm 16:5-6)

When Susie's horizons expanded to become "God-sized," the space within her birth boundaries became large enough for her soul to dwell in security and her heart to rest in peace. In the process she has gained the courage and insight to change a few default settings. Susie did what David suggested as the way to claim a "goodly heritage."

Not everything possible for human beings to experience is necessary to be fully human. Not every desire we feel growing within us must be fulfilled for us to have a desirable life. Not every dream or every aspiration can find a place on this earth. The soul is the home of dreams, and the heart the temple of our desires. The power with which we dream and desire is the power to create happiness within the limits of what is possible and the freedom to challenge the boundaries of what seems impossible.

Whatever boundaries there are in our life, they are *our* boundaries. Through God's grace we can accept those that cannot be changed and creatively realign others. It is amazing what a little spiritual insight can do.

6

I Learned
to Keep My
Own Balances

*H*aving recently lived in the same house for a week with two grandsons, a two-year-old and a one-year-old, I rediscovered a truth long forgotten. For children, going to bed is like the last day of their life. They grieve the loss of the day and resist entering into night's darkness with a fierceness not unlike that of a drowning man who will fight for one last gulp of air even when going down for the last time. Watching them struggle against their own tiredness as they were carried off, I may have learned the inspiration for the poignant lines by Dylan Thomas, "Do not go gentle into that good night . . . Rage, rage against the dying of the light."

Many two-year-old children have not yet learned an emotional attachment to things that do not yet exist—something we call hope. There is no "tomorrow" in the feeling self of a very young child. The feelings of children do not remain attached for very long to something they can no longer see or touch; their feelings are prompted more by present experience. Yesterday and tomorrow provide no compensation and little comfort to a young child, whose world is one of feelings not yet attached to concepts.

Our primal vocabulary is rooted in what we feel before it expands to what we can imagine. Though sleep mercifully prevails, and the night suddenly becomes a dreamscape playground—or sometimes a monster-filled nightmare—the child has little awareness of what lies ahead. Children do not resist sleep because they fear the night so much as because they grieve the loss of the day. Before they develop longings for what has never been, they mourn the loss of what they still clutch in their hands. You will have a difficult time balancing the emotional accounts of a child by replacing a real debit with a promised credit.

Measuring Our Gains and Losses

"When I was a child," the apostle Paul wrote, "I thought like a child, I reasoned like a child" (1 Corinthians 13:11). From our own experience we can gain some insight into what he meant. In a childish way of thinking and reasoning, "a bird in the hand is worth two in a bush," as proverbial wisdom puts it. Promise a two-year-old boy a new toy as compensation for giving up his immediate possession of the TV remote control, and you have added little to balance the scales of justice in his mind. The child's sense of values is weighted heavily in favor of something that provides immediate gratification.

This is rooted in what I described in the first chapter as "infantile narcissism." The intrinsic longing for self-fulfillment comes to expression first as a feeling of gratification when immediate needs are met. The capacity for delayed gratification of these needs for the sake of a more lasting and cherished form of self-fulfillment is one mark of growth and maturity. "When I became an adult," Paul testified, "I put an end to childish ways." As a result, he concluded, "faith, hope, and love abide, these three; and the greatest of these is love" (1 Corinthians 13:11, 13).

These three—faith, hope and love—when realized as deeply held feelings of self-worth and value, serve as positive balances in "keeping accounts" so we do not end up in the deficit column of personal happiness. Despite grievous losses and searing disappointment, Paul had learned to balance his own accounts. He suffered real losses, personal injury, attacks on his character and, most of all, failure to realize his plans to go to Spain to preach the gospel. He chose to balance these losses with gains that could be grasped only by faith, hope and love. To be sure, there were occasional tokens and gifts to meet immediate needs, but these were received by a heart already satisfied that the balance had been tipped in his favor.

Writing from a Roman prison, where he was languishing after being arrested in Jerusalem three years earlier, Paul could say to the Christians in Philippi, "Whatever gains I had, these I have come to regard as loss because of Christ. More than that, I regard everything as loss because of the surpassing value of knowing Christ Jesus my Lord" (Philippians 3:7-8). Responding to their gift of money to meet his physical needs in prison, he added, "I have been paid in full and have more than enough; I am fully satisfied, now that I have received from Epaphroditus the gifts you sent, a fragrant offering, a sacrifice acceptable and pleasing to God" (Philippians 4:18). Their sacrificial gift was only a fraction of what Paul actually needed to sustain his daily life in terms of material things. But his own faith, hope and love were revived via this tangible gift. Moreover, he immediately assured them, "And my God will fully satisfy every need of yours according to his riches in glory in Christ Jesus" (v. 19).

Why Our Values Outweigh Our Beliefs

In their book *Real Life Marriage* Lucy and Dennis Guernsey suggest that marital compatibility depends more on shared values than shared beliefs. Beliefs represent ideas and tenets that we hold to be true with mental assurance and emotional conviction. In the realm of religious beliefs, we may believe that God exists, that the Bible is the Word of God and that biblical teachings are normative for everyday life. Two persons may have quite different beliefs but share common values. Values represent the choices we make concerning spending money, investing time and deciding what will give the greatest satisfaction. Quite often we will express our beliefs in something but contradict or supersede those beliefs by the values we live out.

Charles and Sue are a married couple who share beliefs in the area of their religious and moral life. They grew up in the same Protestant denomination, were married in the church where they both were members and hold strong convictions about traditional family morals. If asked to state their beliefs, they would state them in terms of what they believe to be morally right, doctrinally true and ultimately good. In their daily life as marriage partners, however, they have become increasingly incompatible and unable to communicate their feelings.

Charles is a perfectionist and likes everything kept in order, both around the house and in his personal life. He spends a great deal of time and emotional energy maintaining balance by controlling every eventuality and avoiding unpredictable situations. He feels most secure and happy when he has everything under control, including the behavior of their children and the family budget. He has faith in his ability to provide, as well as in his decisions, judgments and ability to hold things together. He values himself by being the one in charge, and he feels most fulfilled when he receives affirmation for what he has accomplished.

Sue, on the other hand, loves to begin new things and explore new approaches to life. She has an intuitive faith that things will always work out, even though the solutions may not always be apparent. She lives in hope that her unfulfilled dreams will come true and she will someday be happier than she has ever been. She feels comfortable and quite secure with leaving things unfinished while she goes on to something else that offers more challenge and satisfaction. Her values for her children are in what they will become, not merely how they behave. She feels most fulfilled when she can contribute to the lives of others.

Sue and Charles are living in separate worlds. They sing together the creed of their faith but undermine each other with their individual values. In terms of marital compatibility, their values throw their relationship off balance, leaving a deficit that is fast eroding the capital investment of their promised troth. Each tries to balance the budget of the marriage relationship by increasing the investment in his or her own values.

As a pastoral counselor, I feel like a parent attempting to "get the kids to bed" when each is fighting to hang on to a measure of happiness that gets lost when they turn toward the other. They do not want to "go gently into that good night," but "rage, rage against the dying of the light" (with apologies to Dylan Thomas). What will compensate for the loss of the values that have become indispensable to their desperate and immediate happiness? What value can be placed on the scale to balance the loss of these perceived values?

It is surely no help to mouth the words along with Paul, "Whatever gains I had, these I have come to regard as loss because of Christ." We want to know how Paul came to actually feel that the value of faith in Christ balanced the real losses he experienced in his life. How do we give up our childish ways without losing the deepest joys of child-hood? If there is a way, we must find it.

Learning the Value of Faith

By Paul's reckoning, faith, hope and love are the values that make it possible for an adult to let go of childish ways. Take faith. Sue and Charles have a common confession of faith, expressed through a personal belief in God as well as in corporate worship. Ask them about their Christian faith, and they are quick to tell you *what* they believe. Their faith is an important part of their personal identity, acquired in childhood and reinforced through adult membership in the church.

When we ask *how* their faith enables and empowers them to find satisfaction and fulfillment in daily life, however, they draw a blank. Faith does not *abide* for them in the sense that Paul suggested. It's not that their values have no room for faith. It's more the case that their faith does not provide a value sufficient to count when their personal happiness is at stake.

This couple may well end up driven apart by their differing values and find that their marriage is incompatible with those personal values. If they end their marriage, they will pay a high price in family disruption, economic consequences, emotional trauma and, not least of all, living in contradiction to what they both believe the Bible teaches about marriage. The fact that many couples have gone ahead and paid this price indicates the power of what we value in life over and against what we believe. Many have been willing to live in contradiction to their Christian faith—or at least membership in a particular community of faith—for the values they feel can be gained only through such drastic action.

As a pastoral counselor I have found that appealing to what one believes as an argument for maintaining a commitment to a relationship carries little weight. This discovery disturbed and disconcerted me. I had been taught that promises and vows are part of what one holds as a faith commitment and that reminding people of what they believe would give them strong motivation to abide by these commitments. But I was wrong.

I have learned that the most powerful drive for human beings is the need for self-fulfillment, as expressed by a deep longing for life to have meaning and purpose. As children we experience this longing through gratification and pleasure. This is not wrong, in and of itself. We encourage children to respond at the level of feelings of pleasure and self-gratification. This is the beginning of one's sense of value. At this level there is little tolerance for delayed gratification. Any delay or denial of pleasure is met with a feeling of panic and outrage, combined with a resistance that borders on supernatural power. Just try to wrest a muscular three-year-old away from the candy counter in a store!

The search for self and for fulfillment during adolescence and early adulthood is derailed when a belief system is added on rather than developed with regard to personal values. Religious truths can become indoctrination when commitment is required without recognition of personal values. A dichotomy between faith (what one believes) and values (fulfillment of needs) can go undetected for years and cause an imbalance. This is especially true when the religious belief system is accommodated so as to make belief more satisfying and gratifying to the individuals who become adherents. Faith becomes more narcissistic when it caters to people's felt needs to be successful, prosperous and affirmed. Without realizing it, we develop a faith driven by values, where any needed concessions are demanded from the side of faith. We can preserve faith if necessary by abandoning the institutional and formal structures of faith in favor of a "personal" belief system that is not subject to judgment and control by others.

But here is the other side of the coin. Where a faith system remains rigid and demanding without regard to felt needs, faith may be viewed as dispensable. Faced with such demands, many have chosen to abandon all pretense of faith and base their commitments and decisions on the values of self-fulfillment. This is deplored by those who link faith with commitment to absolute moral principles and doctrinal truths that transcend subjective values. The charge of relativism, subjectivism and humanism is leveled against those who choose the values of self-fulfillment over objective beliefs.

There are many Scripture texts that support the dichotomy of faith and personal values. Think of the biblical injunctions to deny ourselves (Matthew 16:24), to hate our own life (Luke 14:26), to put to death the deeds of the body (Romans 8:13), not to please ourselves (Romans 15:1) and to remember that our old self was crucified with Christ (Romans 6:6). Paul admonishes, "Do nothing from selfish ambition or conceit, but in humility regard others better than yourselves" (Philippians 2:3) In Romans 7 Paul can even say, "For I know that nothing good dwells within me, that is, in my flesh" (verse 18).

One strong theological tradition teaches that the human self is hopelessly sinful and without merit unless it is transformed and renewed by the grace of God. Even then, echoing Paul, the grace by which one lives is not one's own life but "Christ who lives in me" (Galatians 2:20). Under the influence of this tradition, self-fulfillment is considered to be rooted in sinful pride, not in authentic human selfhood.

But note that in the very same context in which Paul says that "nothing good" dwells within him, he can say, "I delight in the law of God in my inmost self" (Romans 7:22). And the command of Jesus to love one's neighbor is grounded in the assumed reality of "love of oneself" (Matthew 22:37-40; see also Leviticus 19:18; Romans 13:9; Galatians 5:14). Rather than the self being annihilated by the grace of God, it is renewed in its capacity to value for itself the gifts of God and affirmed as a fundamental value in human love.

In his perceptive book *Life and Faith* William Meissner suggests that a theology of faith and a theology of grace must be accompanied by a psychology of faith and grace. "Grace," says Meissner, "not only alters our theological condition, changing us in reference to the supernatural, but it delves into our very nature and makes contact with the depths of our psychic reality." The psychological aspect of faith is the value of faith to the self as a reality of self-fulfillment; this is both a present experience and a future promise.

In an informal sermon I once read from Matthew's version of the Sermon on the Mount: "Do not store up for yourselves treasures on earth, . . . but store up for God treasures in heaven." I paused for several seconds to see what effect this rendering of Matthew's text might have upon my hearers. Suddenly a woman sitting in the front row with her Bible open exclaimed, "That is not what my Bible says!" I asked her to read what her Bible said, and she read, "Lay up for *yourselves* treasures in heaven." I pretended to be amazed and asked if anyone else had a Bible with that reading. When others began to look at the text for themselves, they all agreed.

It disturbed me to realize that when I read "for God" in place of "for yourselves," only one person heard that as wrong. We have all become so accustomed to the teaching that nothing should be done "for ourselves" that it sounded quite right that we should lay up treasure in heaven for God.

When the apostle Paul came to the end of his life, he said that he had done all things so as to "gain Christ" (Philippians 3:8). He wrote that he was "straining forward to what lies ahead" and pressing on "toward the goal for the prize of the heavenly call" (vv. 13-14). In a final letter to Timothy he wrote, "I have fought the good fight, I have finished the race, I have kept the faith. From now on there is reserved *for me* the crown of righteousness" (2 Timothy 4:7-8).

I am now convinced that we gain the abiding power of faith when what we believe to be true is received into the self as a gift of God that meets the deepest longing for self-fulfillment. Faith does not create its own value over and against the value of the self. Rather, faith transforms the value of self-fulfillment from its childish grasp on what is immediately at hand to the abiding value of what is achieved through the giving over of self to longer-range personal goals.

The "gift of faith" is the power of God's grace that empowers the self to desire what God promises will fulfill a person. The child does not yet have goals beyond what he or she can grasp at the moment. Faith is what connects the hunger of the self to the hope of the self. Without the hunger, there is no fuel to fire up faith. Without the hope, there is no mark on which faith can set its sight. This is why the author of Hebrews could write, "Faith is the assurance of things hoped for, the conviction of things not seen" (Hebrews 11:1). The writer goes on to say that faith brought benefits and rewards to those who possessed it. By faith the ancestors "received approval." By faith Abel's sacrifice was "more acceptable" and he "received approval." By faith Abraham "received an inheritance."

Faith is rooted in the hunger of the self for recognition, for approval and for those values for which the greatest sacrifice is not too much. We learn to have faith when we discover this hunger and dare to hope for fulfillment.

Learning the Value of Hope

Psychologist Mary Vander Goot accurately identifies the source of much unhappiness in contemporary society when she writes: "Today many people are longing for what now seems like an old-fashioned value, a cause, a goal, or an ideal that could be the lodestar of their lives. The emotional evidence of their predicament is their feeling of fragmentation. Their emotions seem to be like echoes without original sounds. They lack a center: they have no direction." There is a hunger necessary for faith. We have all felt it, this longing for fulfillment that lies beyond the horizon of our daily life.

Thomas Wolfe put it as poignantly as words can tell when he wrote: "O waste of loss, in the hot mazes, lost, among bright stars on this most weary unbright cinder, lost! Remembering speechlessly we seek the great forgotten language, the lost lane-end into heaven, a stone, a leaf, an unfound door. Where? When?"

Theologian Emil Brunner speaks of a "sorrow-of-heart" that experiences the disharmony of existence without a center outside of the self. To attempt to organize the self around its own center, warns Brunner, produces what might be called spiritual or psychological health. But without a center to give the self a place of hope in God, this "health" is itself a form of madness or insanity. "To place the central point of existence outside God, who is the true Centre, in the 'I' and the world, is madness; for it cannot be a real centre; the world cannot provide any resting-place for the Self; it only makes it oscillate hither and thither."

We expect theologians to speak of hope, and some have even become known for their "theology of hope" (Jürgen Moltmann, for example). But theologians themselves have been known to have despair and to fall into the "sorrow-of-heart" of which Brunner speaks. I am speaking here of hope not only as objectively grounded in God but as a deeply felt value of the self. I call hope the vision that is seen with the eyes of faith and that is the balance to satisfy the deepest longing of the heart.

While hope must have its center in God, as Brunner suggests, its value must be realized and felt in the heart. When we have discovered the longing that fuels faith and inspires hope, we have learned its value. A faith that does not arise from this unquenchable hunger for life is not faith but fantasy. There is a cosmic disposal for beliefs that have lost their value and been discarded. Without the value of hope, faith can lose its own value and turn back into despair.

We are not born with the value of hope, but it can be learned. Consider Jesus. In his conversation with the Samaritan woman at the well, he said, "If you knew the gift of God, and who it is that is saying to you, 'Give me a drink,' you would have asked him, and he would have given you living water."

The woman protested, "Sir, you have no bucket, and the well is deep. Where do you get that living water?"

Jesus responded, "Everyone who drinks of this water will be thirsty again, but those who drink of the water that I will give them will never be thirsty. The water that I will give will become in them a spring of water gushing up to eternal life." He thus touched the core of this woman's passion, which up till that moment had been indiscriminately poured out in a series of unfulfilling relationships. What others may have seen as promiscuous sexual passion Jesus diagnosed as an unfulfilled thirst for a love that gave back as much as it took.

She cried out, "Sir, give me this water, so that I may never be thirsty or have to keep coming here to draw water" (John 4:1-15). She was certainly practical, though a thirst had been opened up in her that would soon become faith.

In his own life Jesus revealed a consuming hunger for fulfillment that drove him ever deeper into his mission, to go to Jerusalem and present himself as Israel's messiah. When it became clear that this was leading directly to danger, Jesus cried out, "I came to bring fire to the earth, and how I wish it were already kindled! I have a baptism with which to be baptized, and what stress I am under until it is completed!" (Luke 12:49-50). Lord, what we would not give for this single-minded passion of faith!

The author of the book of Hebrews recognized both the hunger and the hope of Jesus when he summoned us to look to "the pioneer and perfecter of our faith, who for the sake of the joy that was set before him endured the cross, disregarding its shame, and has taken his seat at the right hand of the throne of God" (Hebrews 12:2). Jesus learned the value of hope as an anchor for his own soul when exposed to the assaults against him. Without the hunger for an ultimate joy, he would have chosen a more accessible goal and settled for some form of immediate success. He had plenty of invitations and a score of opportunities to do just that. Without hope as the lodestar of his faith, he would have fallen into the shame of despair and been consumed by the very faith that drove him beyond more attainable goals.

Mark this well. Faith is a dangerous and destructive drive without hope to sustain its passion. Temptation's power seems to be in ratio to the power of faith. Even people without faith make promises and are later tempted to break them. But having faith as a deeply felt longing for fulfillment beyond our immediate circumstances means that we can be led astray by fool's gold, which glitters but does not abide. False hope can be the destruction of real faith, as many have discovered to their dismay.

The author of Hebrews writes with pastoral concern, so that those who are awakened to the value of faith may have that faith grounded in a hope that will abide. "We have this hope, a sure and steadfast anchor of the soul, a hope that enters the inner shrine behind the curtain, where Jesus, a forerunner on our behalf, has entered, having become a high priest forever" (6:19-20).

If faith has its value lodged in the self's hunger and longing for life's deepest joy, where do we locate hope? For hope to have value it must also be resident in the feeling self, not merely held in the mind as an abstract concept. If hope is to be a "steadfast anchor of the soul," it must be experienced in the self alongside of faith. For hope to have value it must be more than a statement of what one believes. It must be a resident hope, not an alien hope.

To be sure, the content of hope lies outside of the self—in God, as Brunner has said, and more specifically in Jesus Christ, as the author of Hebrews has testified. It is the *content* of hope on which faith finally rests. Without this content, assured by the very reality of God and made manifest through the life, death and resurrection of Jesus Christ, hope shatters like glass under the impact of the "slings and arrows of outrageous fortune," as Shakespeare so eloquently put it.

But this hope is alien to many people because it does not *abide* in the soul as the counterpart of faith. We must be concerned with the value of hope as well its truthfulness and objective grounding in Jesus Christ.

I believe that the answer is to be found in what we call spirit. Faith arises in the passion of the soul as a longing and hunger for meaning and purpose. This is the value of faith, and it is a driving force that is willing to sacrifice most other values in order to fulfill its need. But along with passion in the human soul is spirit. Spirit is more elusive than passion, for it exists in the self more as a gift than as a ground of being. In the story of the creation of the first human being, we are told that God formed him from the dust of the ground and "breathed into his nostrils the breath of life" (Genesis 2:7). The Hebrew word for breath is the same as for spirit.

The author of the book of Ecclesiastes writes, "Just as you do not know how the breath [spirit] comes to the bones in the mother's womb, so you do not know the work of God, who makes everything" (11:5). In the time of death, the author concludes, "the dust returns to the earth as it was, and the breath [spirit] to God who gave it" (12:7). The human self has a unique spiritual capacity that is directly related to the Spirit of God. It is spirit in the human soul along with feelings that give rise to hope as a value of the self.

When Jesus appeared to his disciples following his resurrection, we are told, he "breathed on them and said to them, 'Receive the Holy Spirit' " (John 20:22). He thus prepared them to have the assurance of their own shared destiny with him as an indwelling Spirit of hope. Peter begins his first epistle by reminding us that God, through his great mercy, "has given us a new birth into a living hope through the resurrection of Jesus Christ from the dead" (1 Peter 1:3). Paul writes that "hope does not disappoint us, because God's love has been poured into our hearts through the Holy Spirit that has been given to us" (Romans 5:5).

From this we can conclude that hope, which is anchored in Jesus Christ as the One who lives and by whom we can have assurance of eternal life, arises in the human self as the Spirit moves within us. There is a created human spirit given by God through the mystery and miracle of birth, but there is also the Spirit of God, or the Spirit of Christ, that is communicated to the self and experienced as the power of spirit within the self.

Abraham Heschel, a Hebrew scholar, suggests that while our passions move us (what I have called the value of faith), it is spirit that gives the direction and goal to the self (what I have called hope).

Emotion is inseparable from being filled with the spirit, which is above all a state of being moved. Often the spirit releases passion, an excessive discharge of nervous energy, enhanced vitality, increased inner strength, increased motor activity, a drive. While spirit includes passion or emotion, it must not be reduced to either. Spirit implies the sense of sharing a supreme super individual power, will or wisdom. In emotion, we are conscious of its being our emotion; in the state of being filled with spirit, we are conscious of joining, sharing or receiving "spirit from above" (Isa. 32:15). Passion is a movement; spirit is a goal.

The value of hope is thus the "filling of spirit," which empowers the self to release the passion of faith toward the goal hope sets forth. This is why I define hope as the vision that is seen with the eyes of faith and that satisfies the deepest longing of the heart. This is why genuine feeling, as for instance sorrow or joy, is not possible without spirit. As Emil Brunner reminds us,

> For such feelings arise only out of or in spiritual connections. A good meal does not arouse joy; it merely gives pleasure; if I eat with joy it is because my spirit is turned in a certain direction, to that which is true, or good, or beautiful, which is connected with the act of eating, as indeed the Apostle is able to say: "whether ye eat or drink, do all to the glory of God." Through joy pleasure is lifted to a higher plane since its subject is understood in a larger context.

Learning to Balance Myself with Faith and Hope

What of Charles and Sue, whose values are so deeply divided as to make their marriage appear quite hopeless? While they have a common set of beliefs, as I suggested, even as to what their marriage vows demand of them, they do not share a common faith and hope with respect to their marriage.

When I encourage them to use the faith they each have to work out a functional and effective marriage relationship, both confess that they feel it is hopeless. Whatever the longings each has for a life that is meaningful and fulfilling, these longings are no longer attached to their common life. Whatever hope each has as a goal for their lives, there is no spirit that inspires hope with respect to the future of the marriage.

As a pastoral counselor I feel like Ezekiel, who, in being shown by the Lord a valley filled with dry bones, was asked, "Mortal, can these bones live?" (Ezekiel 37:3). Note that the prophet was told to say to the bones, "O dry bones, hear the word of the LORD. Thus says the Lord GOD to these bones: I will cause breath [spirit] to enter you, and you shall live" (vv. 4-5). The key to reviving what is dead and without vital life is the quickening power of spirit.

Sue and Charles are without spirit (hope) concerning their common life together. Therefore concerning their marriage they have no hope, and their faith is without passion and conviction. I speak to them of goals, of values that can be achieved only through the sharing of a common task. And metaphorically I breathe what life I can into the dry bones of their marriage. I bring forth the deeper values each hides from the other and expose the secret hopes in which the spirit of each lies concealed.

They tell me that they cannot find happiness in living with each other. I do not doubt that. I ask them when it was that happiness became their personal goal in life, and they cannot remember. Of course not, for this was the happiness that they sought as a child and continue to seek today. They are shocked when I suggest that the purpose of marriage might not be to fulfill their quest for happiness, and that seeking to find happiness in marriage is the quickest way to *un*happiness! They seem puzzled.

Happiness must be more than an elusive ideal that we seek to find via a marriage partner. When happiness becomes a goal in itself and an expectation placed on another person, we are doomed to disappointment. We *should* experience happiness in marriage, as well as in many other experiences and relationships in life. Marriage may be an occasion for the gift of happiness to be received, but it can never be the cure for unhappiness.

Now we are ready to cut away the fantasy that has turned frigid and breathe on the smoldering coals of the spirit to see wherein lies the fire of faith. Even if the human spirit that empowers faith and hope seems to have been extinguished, the Spirit of God can breathe new life into that which appears lifeless and powerless. When life seems to have tilted terribly out of balance, so that feelings are dead, faith lifeless and hope dashed to the ground, the Spirit of God creates what we cannot conceive. Out of barrenness, God's power conceives a new value for our lives. This reality empowers me to believe for Sue and

Charles that all things are possible. With this counsel of God's Word and the creative power of God's Spirit, I expect, like Ezekiel of old, the "valley of dry bones" to shiver and shake.

I must rouse passion and ignite spirit in order for each to discover the power of their values to direct their lives. Can they discover, to their surprise, that they are neither prisoners of promises made wrongly nor forced to drink of a cup where sweetness has gone sour? Is it possible for them to receive gifts of the Spirit and experience love, joy, peace and forbearance (Galatians 5:22-23)? Indeed they can! They can become "inspired" and begin to consider the power of values in their life to affect their goals and choices. They can be empowered to look ahead, like Jesus, not to a cross on which they will be nailed, but to see the "joy set before them," reaching out for the values that balance the burden of perceived losses.

My optimism concerning the power of faith and hope to heal and renew life where it has been damaged is based on the intrinsic power of the value of faith and hope. When I see people risk everything and make enormous sacrifices for the sake of achieving short-term personal values and goals, I know that this power can be challenged and inspired to reach out for goals that belong to what is ultimately most satisfying and rewarding in life, to receive what God gives.

Why shouldn't the passion of faith and the spirit of hope, which have sufficient value so as to cause Sue and Charles to sacrifice their marriage for personal desires, be directed toward a *shared* faith and hope? It requires incredible resources of the human spirit to give up what was once loved and cherished for the sake of a new venture. People do not walk away from their vows because they are bereft of faith, but because the value of their faith has shifted. Where once desire for each other empowered them to find value in their marriage roles, desire has fled, leaving only duty. In the end, desire will always win out over duty, for desire taps the fire that fuels faith and causes hope to be reborn out of despair. Desire, however, must be attached to a vision and goal that can be realized only through sacrifice and commitment. This is not child's play or childish pleasure.

The personal and individual values of Sue and Charles are not the cause of their estrangement. What appears to be a desperate incompatibility is primarily a difference in the way that each seeks fulfillment. If persons tend to marry opposites, as psychologists tell us, it may be that each is seeking a relationship that compensates for his or her own strength in one area and weakness in another. The genius of love is not the luck of the draw, where we find the person "just like us." Rather, love is the core value that offers fulfillment beyond what any individual pleasure or desire can give.

When Charles and Sue begin to see the values that link their destiny together as partners in marriage and family, they will discover the freedom to allow the other to have his and her own personal scale of values. They will experience complementarity rather than competition in their relationship.

When faith and hope become disengaged from our childish grasp on our immediate pleasure and become values that motivate and empower us to pay the highest price for the greatest good, we call that love. And where love abides, as the apostle has written, we have what is greatest (1 Corinthians 13).

Learning the Value of Love

"We no longer love each other," Sue and Charles confess at last.

"Probably you never did," I quickly respond. I meet their protests with agreement. "Yes, I know that you once felt the irresistible passion, expressed in the language of love with words and touch and sealed with a solemn vow to love until death's last breath. But love can't be lost until it is learned. And what feels like the loss of love may actually be the costly separation of self-gratification from self-fulfillment."

Let me explain. The apostle's hymn of love begins with the assertion that "if I have all faith, so as to remove mountains, but do not have love, I am nothing. If I give away all my possessions, and if I hand over my body so that I may boast, but do not have love, I gain nothing" (1 Corinthians 13:2-3). The value of love is so great that without it even the passion of faith and the most supreme sacrifice of life come to nothing.

Lest we assume that love is a mysterious force that borders on the divine, Paul describes it in terms of the most difficult and painful context, where our skin and temper rub together in the narrow confines of a relationship. "Love is patient; love is kind; love is not envious or boastful or arrogant or rude. It does not insist on its own way; it is not irritable or resentful; it does not rejoice in wrongdoing, but rejoices in the truth. It bears all things, believes all things, hopes all things, endures all things" (vv. 4-7).

These are beautiful words, often read at weddings. The value of patience, kindness and giving way to the other must be learned. The practice of love in this range is off the scale for a child's repertoire of response. The learning of love is not the acquiring of skills, such as can be learned through instruction and repetition. What Paul describes has to do with values, not affections or feelings alone.

When I learn the value of patience and kindness, I receive the rarest gift of all, the trust and companionship of another human person. When I learn the value of self-forgetfulness for the sake of enlarging and empowering the life of another, I experience an intimacy and union that touches my own soul to the core until I almost cry, "Enough! How can I bear such joy?"

Charles and Sue, you never learned the value of love so as to experience this gift and joy from each other. Where will you go to find it? And what will you be seeking when you begin your search? Will the conditions be more suitable, more realistic, next time? Possibly. I have known that to happen.

There are occasions when the pain is so unbearable and the wound so deep that before the learning can begin there must be healing. But then let the healing begin at least, and let faith and hope be restored so that love can be produced out of empowerment rather than impoverishment.

The value of love can be measured only by what it costs, what we are willing to lay on the table and trade away for the sake of the transparency and vulnerability of looking another person in the eye and saying, "My soul is bound on this earth to our common destiny. I desire above all else to gain my soul. And I give you your freedom from my deepest needs in order to have my greatest desire."

The value of love is freedom. Not freedom from the tyranny of the demands of others, but freedom to make others free. Anne Morrow Lindbergh, who knew something of pain and loss and no doubt had less happiness than she once dreamed of, learned the value of love and expressed it in the poem "Even":

Him that I love I wish to be
Free:

Free as the bare top twigs of tree,
Pushed up out of the fight
Of branches, struggling for the light,
Clear of the darkening pall,
Where shadows fall—
Open to the golden Eye
Of Sky;

Free as a gull
Alone upon a single shaft of air,
Invisible there,
Where
No man can touch,
No shout can reach,
Meet
No stare;

Free as a spear

Of grass,
Lost in the green
Anonymity
Of a thousand seen
Piercing, row on row,
The crust of earth,
With mirth,
Through to the blue,
Sharing the sun
Although,
Circled, each one,
In his cool sphere
Of dew.

Him that I love, I wish to be
Free—
Even from me.

Well, the grandchildren were put to bed without the freedom to make their own choice in the matter. We provide the balance in their lives. We have faith, hope and love. We are learning to balance the losses with gains, so that on our personal scale we feel that we have come out ahead. In those moments, we pause to count our blessings. Perhaps this is happiness.

7

I Learned to Count My Own Blessings

*A*s a pastor, I am often called upon to bless infants and children following the pattern of Jesus, who, we are told, "took them up in his arms, laid his hands on them, and blessed them" (Mark 10:16). I fully understand the motives of parents who desire a ritual for their children that communicates and consecrates God's touch on these vulnerable lives. I am pleased that Jesus understood the need and took the time to give the blessing. I often wonder, though, whether the child will grow up to "feel blessed." I know some adults who do and who tell me that they feel blessed. But I also know many who do not; for them a prayer and promise seem to have little effect.

It is so easy for me as an adult to bless a child on behalf of God, but sometimes it's very difficult as an adult to feel blessed by God.

One of the hymns that we sang when I was a child, but that has mysteriously disappeared from most modern hymnals, went something like this: "Count your many blessings, name them one by one; and it will surprise you what the Lord has done!" One of the ironies of our age is that in the relentless search for pleasure, so many people end up unsatisfied and unhappy. "Feeling blessed" appears to have disappeared from our hearts as well as from our hymnbooks.

This malady has been called "narcissistic injury" by psychologists. The deep-seated longing for fulfillment of the self's original need for feeling loved and blessed has suffered a wound no self-gratification can heal. Feelings of pleasure can be found for a time through immersion in some activity or experience. But when we have lost the sense of being blessed by another's love and care, the sweetest pleasure flees as it came, leaving us feeling more cursed than blessed.

After surveying the devastation of love and the destruction of hope in his personal life against the backdrop of the Holocaust during World War II, Quentin, the main character in Arthur Miller's *After the Fall*, concludes, "We meet unblessed; not in some garden of wax fruit and painted trees, that lie of Eden, but after, after the Fall, after many, many deaths . . ." Contrast this with a passage I quoted in the previous chapter—the apostle Paul is writing here to the church in Philippi from prison, after experiencing crushing blows to his plans and enduring physical hardships and afflictions for years: "I have been paid in full and have more than enough; I am fully satisfied, now that I have received from Epaphroditus the gifts you sent, a fragrant offering, a sacrifice acceptable and pleasing to God" (Philippians 4:18).

Remember that in 1 Corinthians 13 Paul tells us that he "put an end to childish ways" when he became an adult. I have suggested in the previous chapters that becoming an adult means learning to choose our own boundaries and keep our own balances. I believe that there is a third way to reach the joy and happiness of a fulfilled life, and it comes when we learn to count our own blessings.

It was late in the afternoon, and my two-year-old grandson was becoming increasingly frustrated with a particular toy. It no longer provided the gratification that it had earlier in the day, when he still had a measure of patience. Attempting to rescue him from a rapid decline into despair and self-pity, I brought out a dozen other toys and some of his favorite books and said, "Look, Brandon, you have all these things to play with! You are really a lucky little boy to have so many nice things to make you happy!"

It didn't work, of course. In no mood to count his many blessings, he proceeded to throw them as far away as he could.

Children are a blessing, but they can become hopelessly childish when it comes to feeling blessed. Having a sense of being blessed is perhaps the clearest measure of maturity in our growth toward love. One thing we are sure to discover: it is not a toybox full of toys that makes us feel blessed, but a heart full of gladness and a handful of peace.

The Road Less Traveled
The feeling of being blessed can only be described; it cannot be defined. It is something that we must experience. It cannot be taught, but it can be learned. There's no technique by which it can be achieved, but there is a pathway that leads toward it. It is more a discovery than a discipline.

Years ago, while struggling as a pastor to integrate the demands of ministry with my own personal destiny, I came to a critical impasse. It began to dawn on me that the thought of God's blessing on my ministry had less to do with performing God's work than with living out God's love. In my journal I wrote these words:

For over thirty years I have been pursuing a desperate course with an impossible speed. It is not that I have been misguided—only that I have forgotten to see, feel, touch, and taste. I would not retrace a single step—yet I know that I have scorned a thousand nights in my blind haste. It has always impressed me that Jesus was not pursued nor pursuing. Nothing could interrupt him, nor could anything detain him. He saw every cripple yet passed them up for the cross. He felt every pain of the hungry, the dispossessed, and the sinful, yet had time for his own suffering. There was a time when I would have been satisfied with nothing less than saving the world—now I am more concerned with saving myself. Somehow I think the two are more related than it first appears.

This much I say with grateful heart—my life has merged with my ministry. I no longer fear that my life will take more time than this moment. Sunday night I said this: "If you need more time to find greater happiness—you have placed far too much value on things that are unimportant." The more I think about it, the less I care about anything else I have said. This will stand.

Looking back, these thoughts do not seem so radical. At the time, though, I remember feeling that I had crossed over some threshold and taken an irrevocable step, almost daring God to bless me. If God indeed is love, as I had come to believe with all of my heart, then God existed for me as the love that I accepted as the criterion for all reality—his and mine.

It was about that time that I read "The Road Not Taken," by Robert Frost:

Two roads diverged in a wood, and I—
I took the one less traveled by,
and that has made all the difference.

The "less traveled road" became the blessed road for me.

Several years went by, with a cautious and yet committed approach to exploring and sharing what I called "the great idea." If others were aware of this venture and pilgrimage, they were unable to talk of it any more than I was. Nevertheless, there seemed to be a common knowledge that this less traveled road was indeed a royal road to God's love. A breakthrough appeared to have come with the sudden discovery that what had felt like a daring venture was in reality a divine direction. A proverb stimulated my reflection: "The king's heart is a stream of water in the hand of the LORD; he turns it wherever he will" (Proverbs 21:1).

Perhaps there was a time when the venture was—or at least seemed to be—only a move I made out of desperation. Then the incredible truth dawned on me: my own heart is being guided like a stream into the crevices of others' lives through unimaginable forces and imperceptible sources. A clarity drenched me with wonder and excitement, that my life *is* an instrument of a greater love and a greater idea.

This is what the king knew. This is what only the king could know and thus yield to the sovereignty of that knowledge—yes, to trust. And even more—to be able to share that knowledge with another, or even better, to discover it together, trust it together. From this point on, I began to have the feeling that I could count my own blessings, not in terms of having needs fulfilled but in having no need to be fulfilled beyond the measure of each day's quota of happiness. This is why when I read Paul's closing comments to his friends in Philippi, I sense that he had learned to count his own blessings.

"I have been paid in full," wrote Paul, "and have more than enough; I am fully satisfied." When we can say that, we have learned to count our own blessings. Paul had discovered three ways to do it. Each one can guide us onto the royal road to blessing in the center of God's love.

Receiving All You Have Coming

"I have been paid in full." This would be hard for most of us to admit. Despite what may come to us as either payment for work done or compensation for sufferings experienced, we can still be left with a feeling that life owes us something. Perhaps it is the implied promise in the original blessing received as an infant that never seems to come true. Once a promise is given, a debt is created. The keeping of a promise is payment on that debt.

"Owe no one anything, except to love one another," admonished Paul (Romans 13:8). By this Paul implied that once love is promised, an obligation has been created that only love can fulfill. To claim the promise is to live in expectation that full payment will be received. Likewise, to experience default on the promise is to be feel we have been defrauded of what is rightfully ours.

We are on a healthy track when feelings focus on the expectation that there ought to be compensation for the demands life makes on us. We are seeking a blessing. To bless someone is to open a window through which love shines and creates a wealth of joy and happiness. When we open that window in another's life, we had better be prepared to let love shine on them. This truth is eloquently stated by theologian Hans Urs von Balthasar:

> God, who inclined toward his new-born creature with infinite personal love, in order to inspire him with it and to awaken the response to it in him, does in the divine supernatural order something similar to a mother. Out of the strength of her own heart she awakens love in her child in true creative activity. . . . The essential thing is that the child, awakened thus to love, and already endowed by another's power of love, awakens also to himself and to his true freedom which is in fact the freedom of loving transcendence of his narrow individuality. No man reaches the core and ground of his own being, becoming free to himself and to all beings, unless love shines on him.

Likewise, withholding love for whatever reason violates the promise and clouds the blessing, resulting in an almost inexplicable feeling of being robbed of what is essential to make life meaningful and fulfilling. As James writes, to say, "Go in peace; keep warm and eat your fill," without meeting others' bodily needs, is of no value (James 2:16). This is as much as to say "God bless you" and then close the window on the fingers of the one who reaches out expecting a gift of love.

It is unfair to accuse persons who feel that life owes them something of having a spirit of selfishness or self-centeredness. We must not be too quick to assume that such people are demanding more than they have a right to expect, as though it were a virtue to give of oneself without expecting to receive. I know well the proverbial saying "It is more blessed to give than to receive." Paul attributes the saying to Jesus (Acts 20:35). But we cannot give what we have not already received. Paul's admonition to the elders of the church at Ephesus was part of his farewell address, in which he had already reminded them of the riches of God's grace and the inheritance they had received as children of God (20:32).

One definition of the grace of God calls it "unmerited favor." That is true, but it tends to focus on our undeservedness. To receive as a gift what we have not earned is truly a blessing of grace and an expression of love. At the same time, because grace has its source in love, what love promises when it makes the other an object of love creates in the loved one an expectation of a blessing. We have not merited this blessing, but it is rightfully ours because it has been promised by love.

Think of it this way. We all enter life totally dependent on the intentional care of other persons. More than milk to nourish our physical needs, we need love to make us feel that we belong, that we are, in fact, necessary to the happiness of those who care for us. We did not ask to be born. We exist due to the actions of others, whether intentional or not. In the care directed toward us there is communicated an implied promise, that "I am valued."

The meeting of these early needs, which ensure our survival and growth, unleashes a deeply felt longing to be valued as a person. To be a self, to be of worth in a world of other persons, is to develop an expectation that this implied promise will be fulfilled. Yes, it is true: when love shines on us, it is the pure grace of another's life expressed favorably toward us. Our existence is not of our own will or power; it is dependent absolutely on the intentions of others either to nourish that existence or to neglect and even abuse it. But our existence is also a demand on others that we receive what love has promised and what only love can give. To love another person is to give that person a promissory note that reads, "Pay on demand."

What does this say about God's love? If, as von Balthasar has suggested, the love of God creates in the child something like the love of a mother, then God too has an obligation to fulfill his promise. When we give God's blessing to a child, we are giving that same promissory note.

Yes, I know. This gift of God each person bears—the divine image and likeness—has become distorted. Like our original parents, Adam and Eve, we are broken off at the core of our being from this promise and make impossible demands on ourselves for fulfillment. This original sin traps every person in the vicious circle of nonfulfillment. Despite every effort to make up for the deficit in the self through knowledge and awareness, we still find that we are prone to using and abusing others.

Some, meaning to save us from this condition, tell us that we are worthless, not merely hopeless. Only by denying ourselves, we are warned, can we be accepted by God's grace. We have no merit in ourselves and no right to expect anything of God, so the evangelists tell us.

This half-truth of the gospel of grace can offer the gift of salvation but ordinarily does not result in the full truth of being blessed. Look around the church. It is filled with people who profess God's salvation from sin but are still searching for God's blessing of love. Not having received the blessing promised, many Christians still are looking for the payoff in serving God.

Being blessed means that one has been "paid in full," to use Paul's expression. The apostle knows all too well the terrible consequences of attempting to fulfill his own need for righteousness. He confesses that he became a "wretched man," captive to his desperate desires and the "law of sin" working within him. He testifies to the fact that he was saved from this life of contradiction and chaos by the grace of Jesus Christ. Yet in the midst of this confession he cries out, "I delight in the law of God in my inmost self" (Romans 7:22). At the very core of his being, Paul does not deny or devalue himself. He feels that God has loved him and called him to be a child of God. "We boast in our hope of sharing the glory of God," Paul wrote, and "hope does not disappoint us, because God's love has been poured into our hearts through the Holy Spirit that has been given to us" (Romans 5:2, 5).

The gift of the Holy Spirit is God's payment on his promissory note of love and grace. This is why Paul can say that he has been paid in full.

When I take an infant in my arms to pronounce God's blessing on that life, I am binding God's love to parental love and creating a hunger only the Spirit of God can satisfy. Blessed are those who receive full payment on that promise!

Receiving More Than You Need

Our church fellowship supports a variety of mission organizations and persons in ministry. The treasurer, who is responsible for sending the monthly checks in fulfillment of our commitment, shares with me from time to time the letters received back from the organizations. Invariably the letters acknowledge with gratitude the "full payment" of the monthly commitment and then go on to suggest that there are even greater needs. "Every letter of appreciation," our treasurer once exclaimed, "is really a request for more!"

Contrast this with Paul's letter acknowledging the Philippians' gift: "I have more than enough!" We remember that Paul is writing from a Roman prison and totally dependent on others to provide for the necessities of life. It was customary in those days for prisoners to have their food and other needs provided by relatives or friends. But there is not a whisper of further need in Paul's letter.

Most of us live by the economic rule that our needs rise to the level of available or expected income. In fact, I probably should have said that our needs rise slightly faster than available resources, so that there never is enough. I suspect that for some of us this is true in the spiritual sphere as well. "Thanks, God, but about tomorrow . . ." When Paul considers his life, the column marked "blessings" seems always to add up to more than the column marked "needs." Thus he writes to the Corinthians: "And God is able to provide you with every blessing in abundance, so that by always having enough of everything, you may share abundantly in every good work" (2 Corinthians 9:8).

One of the more poignant passages in the Old Testament is recorded by Samuel concerning David. The king of Israel had taken refuge in a cave from the Philistines, who were garrisoned at Bethlehem. Lonely and isolated, "David said longingly, 'O that someone would give me water to drink from the well of Bethlehem that is by the gate!' " Three of David's "mighty men," hearing him speak, broke through the camp of the Philistines, drew water from the well in Bethlehem and brought it to their leader. "But he would not drink of it; he poured it out to the LORD, for he said, 'The LORD forbid that I should do this. Can I drink of the blood of the men who went at the risk of their lives?' Therefore he would not drink it" (2 Samuel 23:15-17).

As I pondered this story, I wondered how the three warriors felt, having obtained the water at such great effort, to see it poured out on the ground. But then I began to understand. For David to use the water to quench his thirst or to satisfy a moment of nostalgia would have exploited their relationship of heroic devotion and love for the sake of a passing need. Not to use the water to meet a need was, in fact, to acknowledge the blessing of their devotion and to create a blessing for them, a sacrament of thanksgiving.

I later added my reflections on this to my journal notes under the title "An Elegy for God":

From its very conception this gift was doomed
to sprinkle the earth
—was it water or blood?
Too great a need and too much love
conjugate the new verb—a sacrifice presumed
to be a senseless act devouring alike
the giver and the gift.
A crucifixion of logic
upon the tree of knowledge of good
and evil; therein lies a god entombed
too holy to be allowed to live.
Earth drinks in its thanksgiving feast
—is it water or blood?

The finest gifts are not always consumed
upon the parched altars of ravenous thirst.
Renunciation is itself a sacrament exhumed
from eternal immutability: God the dispersed
gathered up again in those who have communed.
Out of all our eucharists, this is the first.

From the very beginning, our longings get mixed up with our needs. When we attempt to fulfill a longing by satisfying a need, the hollow space in our heart grows larger. Blessings belong to longings, not to needs.

For David, as I understand it, the well at Bethlehem was a poignant reminder of a time when his life was unbroken and blessed by the familiar rituals of family and community life. These early experiences can create powerful longings that make us especially vulnerable when we realize that we "can't go home again." Despite some of the unhappy times of our childhood, most of us cling to the feelings we had when we felt most blessed.

So it was for David. The shock of being handed a flask of water from the well at Bethlehem broke through his melancholy musings. Grasping the hands of those who expressed their love and devotion for him, he knew that he had "been paid in full," that he had "more than enough." In pouring out the water, he received the blessing of their devotion, and they in turn were blessed beyond measure by having their efforts consecrated as the water was poured out before the Lord.

Are there not such sacraments of love and devotion in which God becomes real and present to us?

The blessing of God that comes to people when they encounter one another in love is essential to the Jewish experience and artfully captured in a rabbinical story.

Time before time, when the world was young, two brothers shared a field and a mill, each night dividing the grain they had ground together during the day. One brother lived alone; the other had a wife and a large family. Now the single brother thought to himself one day, "It isn't really fair that we divide the grain evenly. I have only myself to care for, but my brother has children to feed." So each night he secretly took some of his grain to his brother's granary to see that he was never without. But the married brother said to himself one day, "It isn't really fair that we divide the grain evenly, because I have children to provide for me in my old age, but my brother has no one. What will he do when he's old?" So every night he secretly took some of *his* grain to his brother's granary. As a result, both of them always found their supply of grain mysteriously replenished each morning.

Then one night they met each other halfway between their two houses, suddenly realized what had been happening, and embraced each other in love. The legend is that God witnessed their meeting and proclaimed, "This is a holy place—a place of love—and here it is that my temple shall be built." And so it was. The First Temple is said to have been constructed on that very site. The holy place, where God is made known to his people, is the place where human beings discover each other in love. The absolute is known in the personal.

How many times have we sent people back to the well in Bethlehem in a misguided attempt to make us happy? How often have we drunk the water to satisfy a craving, only to miss the blessing of a caring heart? We exchange the priceless longing for self-fulfillment for the cheap currency of emotional needs.

But the inflationary spiral of needs propels us into emotional bankruptcy, and we file for "Chapter 11" by retaining the services of a therapist. And if the therapist is wise, she will become a liturgist and, instead of handing us the water to drink, will empower us to pour it out to the Lord and thereby receive the blessing.

We can teach therapists and counselors the skill of finding the well at Bethlehem, but the wisdom of knowing what to do with it when it is found is known only to those who themselves know the blessing.

When longing is fulfilled by love, it is strange how needs diminish.

The most significant step in counting our blessings is to recognize our longings and reduce our needs. Many who succeed in having their needs met are left with unfulfilled longing. The recognition of longing is the open door to present fulfillment, not a narrow passageway into the past. While our longings were created in earlier experiences, they can be fulfilled only in present relationships. But when we are using our relationships to meet our needs, we cannot expect them to fulfill our longings. For what we really long for is not the water from the well but someone to care enough to go and get it. When we have that, we have "more than enough."

Receiving All That You Want

After a recent court trial in which the judge awarded a sizable financial judgment in favor of the plaintiff, who had been the victim of discrimination and sexual harassment in the workplace, the woman was asked by a reporter, "Are you satisfied by the verdict?"

She responded, "I am glad to have the offender brought to justice. But no amount of money can restore the loss of dignity and humiliation which I suffered."

When Paul said that he had been "paid in full" and that he had "more than enough," the most important question—do you have all that you want?—had not yet been answered. The first two statements relate primarily to needs that have been met. The third, "I am fully satisfied," speaks from the deepest longings of the human heart.

"I am fully satisfied," wrote Paul, "now that I have received from Epaphroditus the gifts you sent, a fragrant offering, a sacrifice acceptable and pleasing to God. And my God will fully satisfy every need of yours according to his riches in glory in Christ Jesus" (Philippians 4:18-19). The gift from the Philippian Christians met some immediate needs, "more than enough," but only God can fully satisfy the heart.

"What is it that you women really want?" asked a frustrated male student in a class discussion on gender issues. "You have equal access to power and the same benefits as males in most sectors of our society and in many churches. Yet you do not appear to be satisfied."

After a painful silence, a woman responded quietly, "I long for the day when I will be recognized and appreciated for the person that I am, not only for my rights as a woman."

I felt the class sink into an embarrassed silence. As their teacher, I had to confess that satisfying the deep longings of another person is a tall order for anyone. Moreover, I suggested, for all of our competence and skills in handling interpersonal relations (it was a class in marriage and family relations, after all), we were probably all somewhat uncertain of how to respond at this level.

We are fast moving, I fear, into an era of relationships in which there will be greater benefits with fewer blessings for all. Rights can be legislated and privileges conferred, but the stark reality, as Arthur Miller reminded us, is that "we meet unblessed; not in some garden of wax fruit and painted trees, that lie of Eden, but after, after the Fall, after many, many deaths." We can no longer afford the luxury of pretending we can silence the inner voice that cries out for recognition and belonging by robustly singing, "Jesus paid it all, all to him I owe." The certitudes of Christian faith can be sung with the lips but must also be seized by the heart.

There is no longer a way back to the blessing of Eden, as Miller rightly points out, but there is a way to the blessing of Easter, which lies on the other side of Golgotha. Only when we dare to express our deepest longings can we discover our dearest hope and most satisfying answer.

Along with letters smuggled out of a Nazi prison, where he was confined for activities against the Hitler regime, the German pastor Dietrich Bonhoeffer sent a poem to a friend. Titled "Who Am I?" it reveals his deepest longings:

Am I then really all that which other men tell of?
Or am I only what I know of myself,

restless and longing and sick, like a bird in a cage,
struggling for breath, as though hands
were compressing my throat,
yearning for colours, for flowers, for the voices of birds,
thirsting for words of kindness, for neighbourliness,
trembling with anger at despotisms and petty humiliation,
powerlessly trembling for friends at an infinite distance,
weary and empty at praying, at thinking, at making,
faint, and ready to say farewell to it all?

Who am I? This or the other?
Am I one person today, and tomorrow another?
Am I both at once? A hypocrite before others,
and before myself a contemptibly woebegone weakling?
Or is something within me still like a beaten army,
fleeing in disorder from victory already achieved?

Who am I? They mock me, these lonely questions of mine.
Whoever I am, thou knowest, O God, I am thine.

What is it that we really want? Oh, if we only knew! If we only dared to touch the core of those deepest longings, if we only could find the words to speak. There can be no answer until we ask the question, and there can be no satisfaction until we search out the longing that leads to God.

We are no longer infants who can be taken up into the arms of another and receive a blessing. But our need for the blessing is greater than ever. The search for the blessing is as contemporary as the dawn's light, which exposes the barrenness of this very day, and as old as the plaintive cry of Esau, who sought the birthright he had squandered away for a piece of bread and bowl of stew. " 'Bless me, me also, father!' And Esau lifted up his voice and wept" (Genesis 27:38).

The search for the blessing has become an addictive curse and a captivating cult for many, as Gary Small and John Trent remind us in *The Blessing.*

Some people are driven toward workaholism as they search for the blessing they never received at home. Always striving for acceptance, they never feel satisfied that they are measuring up. Others get mired in withdrawal and apathy as they give up hope of ever truly being blessed. . . . All across the country, cults are holding out a counterfeit blessing to our children. Cult leaders have mastered the elements of the blessing. . . . Providing a sense of family and holding out (at least initially) the promise of personal attention, affection, and affirmation is an important drawing card for many of these cults.

The blessing of God is not limited to one of his children, as in the case of Isaac and Esau, but is open to all through Jesus Christ. The Spirit of God, long promised, has come to all, claimed Peter on the day of Pentecost. Citing the promise in the prophet Joel, Peter announced: "In the last days it will be, God declares, that I will pour out my Spirit upon all flesh, and your sons and your daughters shall prophesy, and your young men shall see visions, and your old men shall dream dreams. Even upon my slaves, both men and women, in those days I will pour out my Spirit" (Acts 2:17-18).

The way to the blessing is now before us. Take these first steps on the path:

☐ Search out the deepest longings of your heart; do not be satisfied until you have expressed these longings to someone you trust, who will hear and understand.

☐ Reach out for the hand of the ones who are willing to "go to the well in Bethlehem" for you; pour out the "water" of self-need in order to consecrate to God the devotion of care.

☐ Drink in the Spirit of God poured out for you; let the longing become a thirst that satisfies all want but is never quenched of desire.

☐ Enter fully into the family of God, the storehouse of what you truly want.

☐ Take up as your own confession the words of David:

The LORD is my chosen portion and my cup;
　　you hold my lot.
The boundary lines have fallen for me in pleasant places;
　　I have a goodly heritage.
I bless the LORD who gives me counsel;
　　in the night also my heart instructs me.
I keep the LORD always before me;
　　because he is at my right hand, I shall not be moved.

Therefore my heart is glad, and my soul rejoices;
　　my body also rests secure. . . .
You show me the path of life.
　　In your presence there is fullness of joy;
　　in your right hand are pleasures forevermore. (Psalm 16:5-9, 11)

Part 3

Everything That Gives Me Happiness Is Shared with Someone Else

8

Beyond Equality to Partnership

The "pursuit of happiness" is offered as the goal of freedom in the Bill of Rights of the United States Constitution, based on the assertion that all persons are "created equal." Since happiness has become an elusive pursuit, more and more of us are turning to a search for equality. While happiness cannot be reached through laws and legislation, equality can—or so we think.

The vocabulary of equality is rapidly displacing the vision of happiness in our society. Fueled by the moral outrage resulting from oppression and discrimination based on sexual orientation, gender identity, ethnic origin, racial characteristics, marital roles, political power structures and economic status, scarcely anyone in our contemporary society is without a cause to undertake and a case to argue. We have become quite familiar with the politically correct phrases: one world, equal opportunity, affirmative action, level playing field, non-discriminatory language and, of course, human rights. In our updated version of the Bill of Rights, the pursuit of equality has taken precedence over the pursuit of happiness.

The collapse of the communist regime in the Soviet Union unleashed a fury of passion for freedom and equality, exposing the virulent conflicts between ethnic groups that had been rigidly suppressed by political and military force under the old regime. Blood flows in the streets once again. The return of freedom of speech and democratic process makes personal happiness and prosperity more valuable but less certain commodities. "We should be happy with the fall of the corrupt party system," one Russian was heard to say in a television interview, "but I look at my children with hardly enough food to eat and wonder what kind of life they will have."

The dramatic destruction of the Berlin Wall made possible for the first time in almost fifty years a united Germany, with East and West Germans now equal citizens and competitors for a shrinking share of prosperity's golden dream. Will each person, having gained equality, also be successful in the pursuit of happiness? We shall see.

As I write, the news from South Africa is encouraging though uncertain. A national referendum has given support to the president's agenda to dismantle apartheid and continue the pursuit of equality within that nation, where three-fourths of the people have been denied citizenship and the vote, based on race and language. With the election of Nelson Mandela as president, a new constitution and government have been installed, marking the end of apartheid as official policy. At the same time there are predictions of even greater conflict and violence as equality becomes a political aspiration and reality.

When equality is held to be the highest ideal and the intrinsic right of every person, a moral power is created that claims the right to question and eventually destroy any structures that deny equality. Here is where conflict can emerge between the moral right to the pursuit of happiness and the moral right of equality.

Some white Afrikaners, for example, claim the moral right to find happiness by protecting their own national, social and religious interests. They have fought bloody wars over this right; some say they are prepared to fight again. In their minds, those who preach a gospel of equality attack the very foundations of law and order grounded in national sovereignty and natural law. The doctrine of equality, they say, is a heretical theology. I myself have heard as much stated by a leading church official in South Africa.

The price people pay for securing private happiness while denying the human rights of others is fearful. It is a happiness full of fear. South African novelist Alan Paton has exposed that tragic contradiction with the incisiveness of a surgeon and the heart sorrow of a poet.

Have no doubt it is fear in the land. For what can men do when so many have grown so lawless? Who can enjoy the lovely land, who can enjoy the seventy years, and the sun that pours down on the earth, when there is fear in the heart? . . . Cry, the beloved country, for the unborn child that is the inheritor of our fear. Let him not love the earth too deeply. Let him not laugh too gladly when the water runs through his fingers, nor stand too silently when the setting sun makes red the veld with fire. Let him not be too moved when the birds of his land are singing, nor give too much of his heart to a mountain or a valley. For fear will rob him of all if he gives too much.

Birthrights and Birthmarks

On a global scale, equality and happiness do not seem to have a common currency. It may turn out that equality is even more elusive as a goal than happiness. The founders of the United States assumed that all persons are "created equal." On that premise rests the foundation of our system of justice and jurisprudence. At the same time we must acknowledged that equality as a personal experience is more of a legal concept than a birth concept. We may be created equal, but we are not created happy.

While we may think of equality as a birthright, we are not equally born into this world. In fact, nothing determines inequality in life as much as our birth. Our gender if not also our sexual orientation, our race if not also our ethnic identity, our status in society if not also our educational opportunity—these are factors and forces that militate against equality as a social reality.

These "birthmarks" ought never become the basis for discrimination. The Bill of Rights guarantees equal protection under the law from any infringement of personal rights. What the Constitution means by this, of course, is subject to a great deal of debate at present.

Happiness is related more to how we succeed in living with our birthmarks than to securing our birthrights. In saying this I must immediately answer an objection. I do not minimize the importance of "equal rights under the law" as essential to our dignity and well-being. Our sense of justice is grounded in this "inalienable right." Happiness, however, is not always achieved when justice is achieved and our rights are satisfied under the law. Some who have achieved equality still have not found happiness.

Equality under the law cannot alone produce happiness. We must add another dimension that reaches beyond the struggle for equality, necessary as that struggle is. Equality is what I as an individual seek in my dealings with others. It is thus grounded in the rights of an individual rather than in the rules of a relationship. Relationship is created by the intention of each person to empower and sustain the life of the other.

A relationship, as we shall see, is not found to be absolutely grounded in equality. This is because equality is essentially an individual concern, while love, the essence of relationship, is the partaking of the value of the other. Where partners share an intention to empower the other, inequality is disarmed of its power to rob the partners of their essential value.

When persons in a relationship such as a marriage, family or friendship seek to achieve equality, even when that is a mutual concern, a certain degree of unhappiness is sure to result. Why is this so?

The Teeter-Totter Syndrome

Our two grandsons, Brandon and Brogan, were playing together on a playground and getting along quite famously despite the fact that Brandon is two years old and Brogan only one. Then Brandon spied a teeter-totter and got Brogan to sit on one end while he climbed on the other end. It didn't work, of course. Brandon was so much heavier that Brogan promptly became marooned high in the air. Disgusted that they could not make it work, Brandon jumped off, sending Brogan down to earth with a crash! Neither one was very happy about the episode, each for his own reason.

Brenda and Allen are on their own teeter-totter. They were married one year before leaving their hometown and moving to another part of the country, where Allen had enrolled in a seminary to prepare for ordination in church ministry. After one year of classes they came to me for some pastoral counseling. They had agreed at the time of their marriage that theirs would be a companionship type of marriage. Each had come from a home in which the husband was viewed as the head of the household while the wife found her role in domestic duties and understood that she was to be subordinate to her husband in spiritual leadership and financial planning.

Brenda and Allen, as university graduates, had been strongly influenced by many of their peers, who viewed such a hierarchical marriage relationship as demeaning to women. Influenced by books that presented a more egalitarian model, they had set out to create such a marriage for themselves.

They believed strongly in equality and implemented this principle in their domestic lives. Both took responsibility for household chores and prepared meals; family budget questions were decided jointly. They had carefully prepared for Allen's three-year studies at the seminary by laying out the longer-range goals for each. By agreement,

Allen would study full time while Brenda worked to support the family. When Allen completed his degree, he would work while Brenda had equal time to pursue a master's degree in accounting, leading to taking her certified public accountant exam. They had carefully balanced their schedules so that each had equal time at work or school, and each was to contribute equally to the household chores.

At the time they came to me for some counseling, they were scarcely one year into this six-year plan. Brenda was the first to speak. She raised a series of complaints about violations of their arrangement: "He goes off to play basketball at the Y with his buddies instead of studying and then says that he has to study at night when we have our only chance to be together." Before Allen had a chance to respond, she went on. "We take turns preparing the evening meal. The one whose turn it is not to cook does the washing up. I don't have time to prepare a big meal on weekdays, as I work until 5:00 p.m. I have to use frozen dishes already prepared or TV dinners. It only takes him five minutes to clean up—which to him means getting everything out of sight as quickly as possible. But when it is his turn to cook, he comes home early in the afternoon and drags out all of the pots and pans he can find and prepares a big meal. Then it takes me an hour to clean up the mess!"

There was much more, of course. Each incident pointed to the imbalance in the relationship as she perceived it, all to her disadvantage.

When Allen spoke, he had no specific complaints but confessed to a pervading sense of depression about their relationship. "It simply isn't working," he said. "We fight about every little thing. I can't seem to make her happy, and I probably have given up trying."

Brenda and Allen's attempt to create an egalitarian marriage on the grounds of absolute equality has resulted in the "teeter-totter syndrome." When the person up in the air jumps off, the other crashes. It requires almost perfect symmetry and a delicate and constant shifting of weight to maintain the balance and rhythm of a teeter-totter. The moment one shifts slightly away from center, the other must compensate in order to preserve balance. This requires constant attention and a great deal of effort merely to maintain the status quo.

A marriage relationship committed to perfect balancing of time, interests and activities means that each day, if not several times a day, there is the possibility of an error. When equality becomes a unit of measurement or a position on a balance beam, the slightest miscalculation can introduce chaos into the arrangement.

The Calculator Crisis

Brenda and Allen also have experienced what I call a "calculator crisis" in their attempt to maintain equality in their marriage. They actually produced for me several sheets of paper with time and task columns plotted out for each person, with a final "balance" line at the bottom showing the exact equality of this division of their life into equal parts. It was to this document that Brenda referred when she pointed out her husband's alleged violations of the agreement. Allen was ready to scrap the entire strategy, but this was taken by Brenda to be further proof that he was trying to sabotage the arrangement so as to gain control in the marriage.

Their experiment had certainly not led to happiness. In fact, from the very beginning it seemed that the happiness they had originally experienced with each other had been eroded. And their trust and respect for each other had already sustained damage.

There are several problems with an attempt to build a happy relationship on the basis of equality. One has to do with power dynamics. All relationships become an occasion for negotiation of power at a certain level. In a traditional, hierarchical marriage, power is assumed to be weighted on the side of one or the other, most often the husband. In this model there is power allocation based on roles and usually gender identity. Where all parties to the arrangement agree to this distribution of power, conflict is avoided because the calculator is in the hand of the one in a "power-up" position.

This is the kind of relationship Brenda and Allen's parents experienced. Allen and Brenda were not aware of the power dynamics in their parents' marriages, because there seldom was a power conflict. There is little possibility of miscalculation in the hierarchical kind of marriage, at least at the everyday level, because the power issue is concealed in the role function. Only when the one holding the power miscalculates so grievously as to cause extreme abuse of the other does power become visible.

When Brenda and Allen attempted to negotiate a more egalitarian marriage, they each picked up a calculator. What they failed to grasp was that they were still operating on the basis of a limited number of units of power in the relationship. They assumed that they could adjust the ratio of power from 60-40 to 50-50 and achieve equality. Their calculation was based on the theory that there was a limited amount of power—100 units—of which each should have an equal share. When their relationship was defined in terms of keeping a balance of power, they were constantly teetering—it would be so easy for one person to throw the other off-balance by getting the advantage, as Brandon did with his younger brother. On the teeter-totter, the boys' weight distribution took precedence over the fact that they were brothers.

This is why Brenda and Allen experienced the calculator crisis. In attempting to distribute units of power evenly so as to create equality, they moved from mutual harmony into "double jeopardy." As in the TV game show *Jeopardy!* each event in their marriage was a challenge to keep score. But in this case the object of the game is to never score more points than your opponent. No wonder the struggle for equality raises anxiety and decibel levels!

The deeper problem here is a misunderstanding of the nature of power in relationships governed by mutual love and trust. When power is viewed as limited in supply, so that one person can end up having more or less than the other, there is a tendency to quantify power in terms of three areas: control of space, control of assets and control of time. These three areas become extensions of self-identity.

The more control we have in these areas, the greater is our sense of power.

The Partnership Paradigm

There is another way of viewing power in terms of personal worth. Each person, created in the image of God, is not created equal to others. Each is equally intended and empowered by God to be a spiritual being with a human nature. We are not human beings with a spiritual nature, but we are spiritual beings with a human nature.

The image of God, in which humans were originally created, is a shared gift of life to be experienced in partnership. In the Genesis 2 account of creation Adam is presented as a solitary person, with no other human beings yet created. At this point God said, "It is not good that the man should be alone; I will make him a helper as his partner" (v. 18). The Hebrew word translated "helper" is used several other times in the Old Testament, referring to God as the helper of human-kind. It is the word we use when we speak of God as our "help and deliverer" (Psalm 70:5) or affirm that our "help comes from the LORD" (Psalm 121:2). When God created the woman as the helper and partner of the man, it clearly did not mean the woman was of less value or importance or that she was inferior in any way. Both were and are equally endowed with the spiritual life that constitutes the image of God expressed through a human nature.

As human beings, Adam and Eve were not equally endowed with the same physical attributes. They were not symmetrical beings—like peas in a pod—but persons with differing natures complementary to each other. Their differences complemented each other and enabled them to share a spiritual partnership as bearers of the divine image.

Because each person is fully endowed with the divine image, each has a "power of being" that contributes to a partner in a relationship. In the same way, when God is seen as the helper of the human person, God can empower him or her without suffering loss of power of his own being.

What does this mean for Brenda and Allen? They are now given the opportunity to revise their view of a marriage relationship and see it as a partnership of empowering rather than a clinic on power division. Their focus can shift from attempting to achieve absolute equality in the functions of their marriage partnership to empowering each other in the roles and tasks that each, by mutual agreement, is free to pursue. Their division of labor and responsibilities can be made on other grounds than calculating equal time and role functions.

Brenda and Allen had attempted to create what Diana and David Garland call a companionship marriage based on egalitarian principles as an alternative to the traditional hierarchical model. The failure of the companionship model of marriage, in the Garlands' opinion, is caused by its excessive preoccupation with self-development, even though the relation is structured along the lines of mutuality.

> The goal of the companionship model is the individual growth and self-actualization of the partners and the growth of the relationship. ... The marriage has no major function except to meet the spouses' interpersonal needs and to enable the individuals to accomplish their own tasks and personal goals. Other functions of the marriage, even procreation, are less significant than the emotional nurture of the partners.

Creative partnership is a better model, suggest the Garlands, because such a marriage focuses on intention and spiritual endeavor rather than on the mechanics of the relationship.

> The goal of marriage based on partnership is not the relationship in and of itself, but pursuit of the purposes of the marriage as the couple has identified them in the will of God. Partnership marriage does not focus on itself, an earthly institution, but strives to transcend itself by focusing on a joint task.... Companionship marriage addresses power distribution; partnership marriage is concerned with the relationship's purpose. Companionship marriage is primarily a focus on structure and process; partnership marriage is primarily a focus on content and intention.

Stanley Hauerwas puts it even more forcefully when he says, "Unless marriage has a purpose beyond being together it will certainly be a hell. For it to be saved from being a hell we must have the conviction that the family represents a vocation necessary for a people who have a mission and yet have learned to be patient."

The partnership paradigm is a step beyond the companionship and egalitarian model, for it implies a purpose that can be achieved only by an intentional commitment to invest equal effort in creating an effective union. The sense of vocation (or calling) Hauerwas asks for challenges each person to contribute something of personal value to the relationship, as a spiritual gift given by God.

With supportive counsel and a new openness with each other, Brenda and Allen can rediscover the spiritual dimension of their commitment as partners who share equally in the divine image and as partakers of the grace of God. The forming of a bonded human relationship, of which marriage is only one instance, involves recognizing the spiritual reality of the other person as well as becoming a partner in a human task.

Partaking in Happiness

After nearly three years with his disciples, Jesus gathered them around him to partake in the mystery of his life being poured out into them. They had become his partners and friends in the spreading of the gospel of the kingdom of God. Now he introduced them to the mystery of sharing in his own life and in the life of each other.

He began by assuming the role of a servant; girding himself with a towel, he washed their feet. The inequality of the arrangement startled Peter, who cried out, "Lord, are you going to wash my feet? . . . You will never wash my feet."

Jesus replied, "Unless I wash you, you have no share with me" (John 13:6, 8).

Later that same evening, he invited them to partake with him in the Passover meal, giving them the bread and wine as a sign of their participation in his life, soon to be broken and poured out. "I do not call you servants any longer, because the servant does not know what the master is doing; but I have called you friends, because I have made known to you everything that I have heard from my Father" (John 15:15).

The apostle Paul, reflecting on this mystery of divine condescension, wrote of Jesus, "Though he was in the form of God, [he] did not regard equality with God as something to be exploited, but emptied himself, taking the form of a slave, being born in human likeness. And being found in human form, he humbled himself and became obedient to the point of death—even death on a cross" (Philippians 2:6-8).

The key to happiness is being in a partnership motivated by love. Where mutual partaking in the spiritual reality of love is not present, happiness disappears, and inequality produces competition and abuse. Paul wrote to the Corinthians when they were out of balance in their relationships to one another, competing over spiritual gifts and vying for places of honor. He first scolded them for their outrageous behavior and then counseled them to consider what it meant to share in the life of Christ as the paradigm of their own fellowship. "Because there is one bread, we who are many are one body, for we all partake of the one bread" (1 Corinthians 10:17).

In using the metaphor of the human body, Paul pointed out that not all members of the body are equal. Some are "weaker" than others but may be more "indispensable" to the life of the body (1 Corinthians 12:22-23). Some of the internal organs, for example, are never visible and have no cosmetic value. When a man begins to lose his hair, he often suffers a blow to his pride and self-esteem. Nevertheless, while a full head of blow-dried hair may add to his power image, losing it is not as serious as, let's say, losing the pancreas.

Paul's point is that we must be careful about measuring the value of the various parts of the body as though each were a single unit. When we do this with the body of Christ, Paul says, we create dissension and conflict.

The solution is to live together so that "the members have the same care for one another" (1 Corinthians 12:25). This is what I mean by empowering each other. Each person, while not equal to others at all points, has a full share in the life and purpose of the relationship. Each is equally valued as necessary to the relation, despite differing levels of participation.

Each Sunday, following our church's worship service, I have to pack up the articles and utensils brought from our home to be used at our temporary worship site. The Communion chalice and bread plates, along with a small tape recorder and my Bible, are placed in a basket. Faith, a three-year-old, likes to help. She places the utensils in the basket with care, and when it is full she wants to help carry it out to the car. The basket, by this time, is much heavier than she can lift. I take one of the handles and she grasps the other; together we carry it out.

There is obvious inequality in the process. Faith accepts the fact that it is my responsibility to decide where things go; she well knows that I am stronger and so can carry much of the weight as well. But I am able to convey to her a sense of being a full participant in the process. The differential in responsibility and strength is artfully concealed so that she has a full share in the task. Her sense of satisfaction and fulfillment is fully equal to mine. Indeed, it probably exceeds mine.

As she grows, the differential will diminish, and she can assume more of the responsibility and carry more of the weight. But her level of self-fulfillment, and may I say her happiness, will not be expected to grow in proportion as she gains equality. She is experiencing even now the deep satisfaction of fully partaking in the special relationship that we have in sharing this task.

I wish it were always so simple. The special care that I take so that our inequality at certain levels is not a barrier to our relationship seems instinctive because she is a child. As parents do with their own children, I feel fulfillment and joy in empowering her.

I must confess that it is much more complicated and difficult with adults. With those who are stronger, wiser or have more power than me, the inequality between us becomes almost a visible barrier. I know I have used my own power to keep certain situations and persons "under control." When I find myself doing that, I realize that I'm functioning as a human person and not as a spiritual person with a human nature.

The society in which we have formed our identity has a tendency to shape us in its mold. Our differences divide us, and the inequality we feel at every hand diminishes us. It is easier to allow a small child behind the walls we have built up, because we still retain the assurance of our own strength and power. It is more difficult to be the child and allow another to carry the greater share of the load for a time.

I have discovered that there are spiritual resources available to us in learning how to live with our human nature. I am rediscovering what it means to be a child of God. Through Jesus Christ, God has artfully concealed the inequality so that I can fully partake in the divine love and grace that flows through his strong hand. Our lives (and our relationships) are like the basket with two handles—one for me and one for God. I am amazed that I can carry my share and receive the full joy of walking with God. This is a partnership that has no equal.

9

Beyond Partnership to Intimacy

*A*s a boy growing up on a farm in the Midwest, I spent many hours alone, often in the fields with the animals, but also choosing my own special places to spend some hours. In those experiences, I recall a feeling of wonderment and a sense of timelessness.

The membrane that separated my inner self from the larger world that pressed in on me grew porous. The familiar sights and sounds that filled my everyday world had cracks in them through which the vast and mysterious unknown breathed upon me, filling my soul with a knowledge for which there were no names and a language for which there were no words.

I still can hear, if I listen, the cry of wild geese winging their way across the night that awakened this small boy and left him staring into the dark, not wanting them to fly out of hearing. But after they disappeared, I lay there wondering what to do with the infinite silence they left in their wake.

There are special silences that break in on the ordinary absence of sound and feel to the soul like the whisper of God. The words are gone, we never heard them, but the silence tells us that they were spoken. I cherish that silence, for it is the temple in which I commune with God in wordless wonder. When he does speak, the silence will have prepared the heart to hear and the soul to sing. A great singer, said Kahlil Gibran, is one "who sings our silences."

There are moments when the ominous roll of approaching thunder and the stabbing brilliance of lightning have filled me with a terror so sweet that I crave, to this very day, the taste of awe-inspired fear on my tongue.

On a cold winter morning, with a rifle cradled in my arm, I suddenly confront a red fox surprised by my silent coming. Crouching only a short distance away, beside a snow-covered shock of corn, the creature stares into my eyes with a fear that I come to understand as that which binds us together for that brief moment. Only when I finally shuffle my feet is the animal released from the compelling power of that common knowledge and free to bound away. The gun is never raised; my aim no longer is to kill.

In what must not be considered sheer sentimentality, I find myself coming full circle to some of these core experiences, some of which now seem to have found a home. On the occasion of the birth of Nathan, the son of my granddaughter Lara, I dipped into this sacred pool of untold experiences and wrote these lines.

> There are rolling hills toward which I glance
> where prairie winds move the grass to dance
> in celebration of sacred vows,
> the rooted rhythm of a chlorophyll chorus line,
> quite oblivious to the roving advance
> of the grazing cows.

I choose the leeward side of the sloping hill
and lie where the close cropped grass still
smells sweetly of bovine breath;
I stanch the bleeding of the severed grass
with my cheek, and promise never to kill
what lies this side of death.

A spirit from the depths of God's eternity
stirs the stillness of what is yet to be,
a birth to bless this temporal place;
I feel the touch of an infant's breath
brush 'cross my cheek, and rise to see
myself in his boyish face.

Thrice removed by each generation
our lives are linked by each separation,
we meet in those we love;
For you, my son, I've claimed heaven's promise
and embraced on earth the joyful consummation
of God's gift from above.

The wind visits the same green hills, if by chance
the cows still graze and the grass will dance,
but the boy has left his lonely station;
when you see his face in your own reflection
you will recognize in his knowing glance
that you are NATHAN!

John Bradshaw, a contemporary popularizer of psychological healing, calls the essential self the *wonder* child within us. This is his way of describing the core of spirituality and the bearer of the image of God within each person. Some psychologists speak of the self as *ego,* while others refer to the self as *soul.* When the term *ego* is used, it refers primarily to the limited sphere of self-consciousness; it is the time-bound self and is rooted in the self's experiences, including family of origin as well as culture. When the term *soul* is used, it refers to more than the ego. The *soul* is the essential self, that core of the self that goes deeper than the ego.

Bradshaw calls the soul the wonder child, while he calls the ego the wounded child. In his view the source of self-fulfillment is the wonder child. The ego, as the wounded child, must be healed in order to allow the wonder child to reach its full potential.

By whatever name, the core self is an experiencing self. If it is helpful to some to speak of this aspect of the self as the "child" within us, I have no quarrel. My own approach has been to trace out the growth of the childish self to the adult self, following the pattern suggested by the apostle Paul. It is in putting away "childish ways," says Paul, that maturity comes (1 Corinthians 13).

The experiences of which I have written above, though received into the self as a child, are not the child within me. These are not childish experiences that are expected to pass away. Rather, these are inarticulate experiences of the self through which the self grows into its maturity. Gibran says it poignantly: "When you long for blessings that you may not name, and when you grieve knowing not the cause, then indeed you are growing with all things that grow, and rising toward your greater self."

When Intimacy Becomes Addictive

I have suggested by the title of this chapter that we must move beyond partnership to intimacy. There is a pseudo-intimacy that can take the place of true intimacy. There is a superficial intimacy that can be taken for real intimacy when our relationship with another person feels powerful and compelling in the moment but has no continuity or endurance.

We must not see intimacy as an end in itself. True intimacy does not become possessive and demanding. If this happens, the need for intimacy becomes an addiction. Then we use relationships with others to feed this need.

Some relationships are not expected to be intimate. In friendship, marriage and family, however, intimacy is ordinarily expected at some level. By "true intimacy" I mean a sense of deeply felt closeness, of being bound together in such a way that sharing space and time with each other is as natural as it is for each person to be alone.

There is a sense in which intimacy belongs first to a person's inner life before it is a factor in relationships. True intimacy begins with an integration of self; one feels comfortable with oneself. In this way intimacy is grounded in the *experiences* of the self rather than in the *expressions* of the self. The inarticulate experiences of the self, as I have suggested above, are not merely childish; in that case when we grew up we would have been able to express them clearly and accurately. Depth experiences will always be inarticulate—that is, incapable of being fully expressed in words and actions.

The apostle Paul reminds us of this when he suggests that receiving the Spirit of God is quite different from knowing the spirit of another person. The Spirit of God "searches everything," Paul writes, "even the depths of God." The human spirit is not capable of such searching and revealing. "For what human being knows what is truly human except the human spirit that is within? So also no one comprehends what is truly God's except the Spirit of God. Now we have received not the spirit of the world, but the Spirit that is from God" (1 Corinthians 2:10-12).

There are many ways we can express the intimacy we may feel when we are close to another. But we can never really share the *same* intimacy any more than we can share the same spirit within us. We are spiritual beings who have a human nature. The spiritual core of our being is personal and unique to each one of us. Each of us then has an experience of the self as a spiritual reality that differentiates us from every other. There is no way I can overcome this difference so as to enter fully into the spirit of another. Nor can I, however much I may wish to do so, give over my spirit to the spirit of another.

In a quite paradoxical way, intimacy is the intensification of *otherness* in personal relationships. Through intimacy we become more aware of the other as the unique and special person that he or she is.

Suppose you are walking on a mountain trail, with no other person in sight. Suddenly you spy a movement across the valley on a distant trail. From this distance it's impossible to tell whether it is an animal or a human. As you close the distance, though, you become aware that the figure is another person. That is, you recognize in the other a likeness to your own human figure, though you can't as yet tell whether it is a woman or a man. At this point you perceive the other as the *same* kind of creature that you are, with no basis for differentiation.

As the other person moves closer, you see that it is a woman and not a man. You become aware of many differences between you in appearance, though you are still excited about the opportunity to meet another person who shares human features. As it happens, when you meet, there is an encounter that leads to the sharing of names, backgrounds and experiences, revealing aspects of the other person to you and you to her.

Then it happens quite unexpectedly and without warning. In a pause in the conversation, while sharing the sense of closeness of two persons whose paths have crossed quite by accident, there is an almost painful sense of vulnerability and openness of spirit. For example, one may say to the other, "I came up here to get away from people. Now I realize that I was running from myself, not others. I really need a friend today!"

With this self-disclosure, a threshold has been crossed. More than a hiking companion, this other person, who was but a stranger a few minutes ago, has now entered into the circle of your personal life. The mutual openness of spirit is quite unexpected but powerfully present. The awareness of the self of the other as absolutely standing over and against your own self is like an electric shock. Shared experiences that seemed merely to draw two people together as having something in common now reveal a confrontation with the mystery and spirit of a self that is totally other than one's own self. The intimacy of communication and communion intensifies the *otherness* of each.

Writing to his friend from a prison cell, Dietrich Bonhoeffer, the German pastor and theologian, reflected on a quotation from Giordano Bruno that stuck in his mind: "There can be something frightening about the sight of a friend; no enemy can be so terrifying as he." Bonhoeffer added: "Does 'terrifying' refer to the inherent danger of betrayal, inseparable from close intimacy . . . ?" There is indeed something "terrifying" as well as exhilarating about the encounter with another whose spirit is open to yours. When this moment of vulnerability and exposure to the spirit of another occurs, it is an unavoidable experience of intimacy. Often we are not prepared for it and shrink from its implications. Or we can become addicted to such encounters and seek the thrill of intimacy for its own sake.

The power of direct contact with the otherness, the spirit of another, can be a compelling stimulant for the psyche. Some become addicted to this stimulation and compulsively seek out encounters, feeding the addiction by disclosing and exploiting the unclothed spirit of another. This can be a dangerous temptation for those who become professional therapists and counselors. Under the mantle of offering healing and hope to those whose spirits are wounded, some counselors secretly fulfill their own intimacy needs by promiscuously finding stimulation in exposing the naked self of their clients.

The search for intimacy, however, is not a craving exclusive to professional therapists. In our generation and culture, a new social disease has emerged that I call intimacy deficiency syndrome. Acquired in adolescence, the disorder runs rampant through restless teenage youth, whose emotional starvation drives them to find stimulation in instant sex and designer drugs. Graduating into young adulthood, these same youths find a culture prepared for them, with self-styled gurus dispensing the latest guides to self-fulfillment by searching out, at all costs, relationships where the intimacy addiction can be fed, if not cured.

There is a subtle temptation in joining support groups that are focused on particular personal needs. While support groups can be indispensable aids to growth and recovery from addiction, the group may use intimacy as the glue that holds it together. My warning here about the addictive nature of intimacy, when sought for its own sake, is intended to keep support groups healthy and conducive to growth.

The craving for intensity in relationship may dull the senses for the enduring quality of commitment to another. Where a relationship does not yield increasing high-intensity voltage, it can be discarded in hopes of finding another. The need for excessive stimulation is one sign of intimacy deficiency syndrome. It is one factor, at least, in the pattern of "serial monogamy" some sociologists describe. This occurs when persons have a succession of marriage partners, divorcing when one marriage fails, moving quickly into another and so on.

The same syndrome may also account for the compelling hold that some cults have on their adherents, especially the young. By offering a high-intensity communal life experience and demanding spiritual defenselessness, the cults thrive on those whose intimacy needs are deficient. By the same token, some churches flourish and expand rapidly when offering a highly stimulating experience of fellowship and worship. Intimacy deficiency may well become a powerful force to exploit for evangelistic purposes. But this will also demand a "high-voltage" Christian experience to maintain the degree of stimulation necessary.

The Recovery of Intimacy
The solution to this problem is clearly not to feed the intimacy addiction but to recover the true meaning and experience of intimacy. The stimulation of a direct encounter with the spirit of another person (as also with the Spirit of God) must not be confused with true intimacy. True intimacy is not the exposure of one's own spirit—or that of another—but the binding of one's spirit with

another as a companion in the task of life.

The core of intimacy is the experience of the self in relation to all that is encountered in life. These experiences, as I have suggested, are inherently inarticulate. They cannot be expressed in the same form in which they have been experienced. This is why attempting to share a deeply personal experience with another person often leads to a temporary suspension of mutuality. While the one articulates an intense experience, the other must wait for a turn. We have learned that it is tactful and necessary not to intrude on such a "sharing," not to voice our own experience until we are free to do so. And true mutuality (intimacy) may often be deepest when people make no attempt to articulate a feeling but simply share the moment.

The experiences I recounted at the beginning of this chapter are noteworthy in that they were not shared with other persons at the time. In retrospect, I feel that my intimacy needs were nourished as my spirit grew and developed through my own encounter with my world. It is true that this took place in a context of supportive and affirming relationships, primarily my parents and siblings. Belonging was felt long before my individuation was secured. At the same time, as I look back I see that my parents were secure in their own individual intimacy needs and thus able to free me to develop my own self rather than be a stimulant to fulfill their needs.

We do experience many things where other people are involved. But because no experience is shared by others in quite the same way, it cannot become a primary building block of the relationship. One time I attended a movie with a friend. At the end he came out of the theater quite ecstatic. To hear him tell it, that single experience had transformed his life, and he wanted me to share in that experience. Truth to tell, the film had left me unmoved, but I think I had the good sense not to say that. Sometimes we must show restraint when it comes to sharing an experience, forgoing the freedom to tell the truth about our own experience for friendship's sake.

Furthermore, we are not morally bound to our experiences. My wife recalls how inspired I became at a particular event we both attended, so impressed was she with my reaction at the time. But now, years later, I don't remember it that way at all. Whatever the stimulation of the experience at the time, it has since lost its intoxicating power in my life. We are quite free to alter our experiences without being charged with betrayal.

If there is a sense of abandonment when a mutual experience is not remembered by each in the same way at a later time, this may be evidence that the experience did not produce true intimacy. Sometimes this leads to pseudo-intimacy, which is not based on trust and openness. This kind of intimacy was not only superficial at the time but also has no binding promise and purpose for the future.

Without a relationship that permits us to be bound to another spirit, we are spiritually homeless. At the same time, that which binds one spirit to another must leave "spaces in the togetherness," as Gibran has so eloquently said.

But let there be spaces in your togetherness,
And let the winds of the heavens dance between you.
Love one another, but make not a bond of love:
Let it rather be a moving sea between the shores of your souls.
Fill each other's cup but drink not from one cup.
Give one another of your bread but eat not from the same loaf.
Sing and dance together and be joyous, but let each of you be alone,
Even as the strings of a lute are alone though they quiver with the
   same music.
Give your hearts, but not into each other's keeping.
For only the hand of Life can contain your hearts.
And stand together yet not too near together;
For the pillars of the temple stand apart,
And the oak tree and the cypress grow not in each other's shadow.

Blessed Be the Tie That Binds

"Blessed be the tie that binds," began a hymn of my youth. While its focus was on "our hearts in Christian love," the third stanza reads, "We share our mutual woes, our mutual burdens bear." The companionship of spirit we seek as a form of self-fulfillment cannot come through intimacy alone but comes through a shared task in life, one that produces authentic friendship.

The tie that bound Jesus to his Father in heaven was not only the intimacy he experienced but also the work the Father was doing through him and the task the Father had given him. While the twelve disciples were called into close fellowship with Jesus, it was the priority of his mission that drew them together when others began to fall away.

Those closest to Jesus had little understanding of the nature of this mission. All they knew was that he was compelled to follow the will and purpose of God. There were many activities as part of this mission. The disciples were his companions and helpers in healing the sick, casting out demons, proclaiming the good news of the kingdom of God and feeding the hungry. At times they were in common danger, such as when they were caught by a storm on the sea, and they shared both the religious leaders' rejection and the welcome of grateful crowds.

What bound these disciples to Jesus was not a shared experience in which each had the same feelings, but a task he shared with them. There were obviously several levels of intimacy among the Twelve. The experience on the mountaintop, where three disciples saw Jesus transfigured and talking with Moses and Elijah, is one example of the special relationship that Jesus had with James, Peter and John.

As Peter became caught up in his own experience of this phenomenon, he blurted out, "Lord, it is good for us to be here; if you wish, I will make three dwellings here, one for you, one for Moses, and one for Elijah."

But this was apparently not intended, and a voice came from heaven: "This is my Son, the Beloved; with him I am well pleased; listen to him" (Matthew 17:1-5).

When Jesus and his friends came down from the mountain, they were confronted by a father and his son, who was possessed of a demon. The task of healing and deliverance became the primary concern, and we hear no more about the shared experience on the mountaintop. Whatever their level of intimacy, the mission of Jesus took priority.

Near the end, Jesus told his disciples that he now considered them his friends rather than servants. This was, as he said, "because I have made known to you everything that I have heard from my Father" (John 15:15). He drew them beyond partnership into intimacy and beyond intimacy into friendship. He did this by sharing with them his own mission and making them companions of his own life journey. He bound their spirit to his own, and his spirit was bound to the mission of God.

The recovery of intimacy is found in the reviving of our own spirit and the binding of that spirit to a shared task. The self, with its deep capacity for intimacy, needs to find a friend. "It is not good that the man should be alone," said God of Adam when there were no other creatures and no other human being (Genesis 2). I suspect that Adam could experience the intimacy of his own spirit in communion with the Creator and the created world. What was lacking for him was a friend, another who shared the capacity for relationship, which leads to companionship of spirit. That was Adam's real need. Friendship makes visible the image of God as a spiritual reality expressed through human beings.

The apostle Paul never went alone on his missionary journeys. From the very beginning he drew others around him and developed a deep companionship with them. When Barnabas left him over the issue of John Mark, he promptly recruited Silas (Acts 15:36-40). His letters from prison note those who were there with him and, in some cases, are appeals for others to join him. In one of the most poignant of his letters, and apparently the last that we have, Paul wrote to Timothy listing those who had left, saying, "Only Luke is with me.

Get Mark and bring him with you, for he is useful in my ministry." He then added a postscript, "Come before winter" (2 Timothy 4:11, 21).

True companionship that leads to friendship revolves around common interests or common tasks, not meeting each other's emotional needs. Mutuality of experience and feelings is not yet companionship in the deeper sense. Companions walk a common pathway and often share a common meal. But it is the path and the meal that provide the focal point for the relation. The sharing of intimacy does not always lead to trust and loyalty. Friendship demands these qualities.

The word *companion* as used in the Bible suggests relationships that involve a high degree of trust, loyalty and shared life. This is what I have called friendship. Jesus refers to David's companions when he describes the removal of the bread from the altar (Matthew 12:3-4; see 1 Samuel 21:6). In his farewell talk to the Christians at Ephesus, Paul reminds them, "I worked with my own hands to support myself and my companions" (Acts 20:34).

Not all companionship is profitable or edifying. There is a companionship of fools and one of gluttons (Proverbs 13:20; 28:7). "Bad company [companionship] ruins good morals," warns Paul (1 Corinthians 15:33). The human need for companionship is a powerful magnet, drawing people together for both good and evil.

The psalmist tells the Lord, "I am a companion of all who fear you, of those who keep your precepts" (Psalm 119:63). The companionship that belongs to those who share the Spirit of God has resulted in one of the most remarkable demonstrations of human fellowship in history. For nearly two thousand years, across oceans and continents, bridging culture, race and language, the bond between Christians who are partakers of the Spirit of Jesus Christ has created spiritual kinship among people who otherwise have little in common. This is what Jesus meant when he called his disciples friends.

We are spiritual beings who also have a human nature. The compelling power of friendship is the hunger of the spirit for a "soul mate." When we have found such a person, we experience the fruit of intimacy. When intimacy is sought only for its pleasurable effects in relationship, it bears no fruit. Intimacy is the fruit that comes from genuine openness of being, one to another. When we move beyond intimacy for its own sake into friendship, intimacy is the gracious gift in the relationship, not a compelling drive.

The biblical story of David and Jonathan is an example. Jonathan was the son of King Saul and the next in line for the crown. But Jonathan "loved David as his own soul," and they made a covenant of friendship that endured to the end (1 Samuel 18).

I did not spend all of my childhood time alone, pondering the mystery of life, as described at the beginning of this chapter. The days of my boyhood on the farm were spent, for the most part, sharing in the tasks that filled the lives of every member of the family. I spent many days working alongside my father, who rarely spoke of his feelings or inquired about mine. I was given to understand that our destiny was largely determined by the efforts we put into working the farm, along with the unpredictable and uncontrollable elements that as often ruined our work as rewarded it.

In light of today's preoccupation with intimacy as the communication of feelings and the disclosure of innermost thoughts, our family would have been considered dysfunctional, I suppose. We never thought so, and to this day I will not believe it. We were drawn beyond the intimacy each treasured as our own gift of life into a depth of love and friendship that in turn became a bond I can only call blessed.

Is this happiness? You bet it is! True intimacy only lasts when it is shared with a friend. When you find the friend you will find the path.

You show me the path of life.

In your presence there is fullness of joy;
in your right hand are pleasures forevermore. (Psalm 16:11)

10

Beyond Intimacy to Friendship

*O*nce certain words have been used to strike terror in the heart, they never regain their former innocence and neutrality. "Ray! The cows are in the corn!" my mother would call out on a peaceful August afternoon, breaking into my self-indulgent lounging in the shade of the house while I was supposed to be herding the cows. The pasture had been nibbled to a nubbin of grass, but the roadsides offered a luxuriant feast to the hungry cows. With no fences to contain them, they had to be carefully watched lest they trespass on the nearby crops.

The cornfield was especially tempting. Tall green stalks, each with its own immature but succulent ear of corn, awakened forbidden fantasies in the right brain of the bovine creatures. Apparently these animals had inherited a subconscious taste for the delicacy and could sniff out self-fulfillment a mile away.

"The cows are in the corn!" What terror struck my soul when I heard those words—not only because the cry signaled a serious failure to heed my sworn duty to keep watch over the animals lest they destroy the valuable crop, but also because I knew from experience how difficult it would be to get them out of their field of dreams. Only someone who has stared a crazed cow in the face, with the green drool of half-chewed cornstalks dripping from its jaws, will understand the nature of the task.

These animals were friends of mine. In a normal state of mind they permitted me to nudge them one way or the other and, if their bellies were full, to climb up on their backs and ride them partway home. But on this day there was no recognition in their eyes. As they wallowed in an orgy of sensual delight, their wildness overmatched my will. Only my panic caused sufficient adrenaline to flow, enabling me to drive them out and corral them safely in the dry-as-dirt sanctuary of the barnyard.

Thankfully, the conscious memory of cows appears to be short. At milking time that evening they came innocently and quietly to their stalls, in utter denial of their earlier romp in the corn.

To this day, if you wish to rouse me to utter panic, simply cry out, "Ray! The cows are in the corn!" They say old fire horses always get excited when they hear the fire bell. The same is true of old cattle herders.

From Self-Indulgence to Self-Fulfillment

The story of the cows in the corn is a parable of the power of self-indulgence allowed to run rampant. Without restraint, self-indulgence among human beings can be just as chaotic and crazy. The original temptation in the Garden of Eden was a powerful enticement to feast on forbidden fruit, not because of a craving for the fruit but because of the sensuality of self-gratification. "When you eat of it," the serpent said to the woman, "your eyes will be opened, and you will be like God, knowing good and evil" (Genesis 3:5).

The temptation is powerful, for it speaks to the original longing for fulfillment placed in human beings by the Creator. As spiritual beings we have a human nature. The self is created in the image and likeness of God. This is a spiritual dimension of existence that reaches out for more than human nature itself can provide.

Thus the basis for that original temptation is not something in the human nature that is opposed to the spiritual nature. Humanity is not a restraint that God placed on our spirit to keep it in check, like a fence to keep cows out of the corn. Human nature is a limitation placed on the extension of the self in time and space. But this limitation does not apply to the spiritual reach of the self in the search for a true "soul mate."

Only the spirit of another can define and fulfill the self. This is why in the second chapter of Genesis, God said of the solitary person, "It is not good that the man should be alone" (v. 18). Only when the woman was created and the two could confront each other as spiritual beings with a human nature was there true fulfillment: "This at last is bone of my bones and flesh of my flesh" (v. 23).

The intimacy produced by the openness of one's being to another is the fulfillment of a deep longing. It is this intimacy that takes us beyond partnership. Intimacy is a personal experience that one receives out of the relationship, and there is a strong sense of fulfillment when the intimacy need is met. But the spiritual dimension of the self is not satisfied with mere intimacy.

There is a longing created in the human soul that intimacy can never fulfill. This is not a "God-shaped vacuum," as someone once said. It is not an empty space within the self but the *life* of the spirit reaching out to be touched and to touch the spirit of another. Of course, God as Spirit is the ultimate and essential Other who alone can fulfill this spiritual dimension. As spiritual beings with a human nature, however, we reach out for fulfillment in the direction of "bones and flesh," as Adam originally put it.

Self-fulfillment is an intrinsic need and a positive good for every person when defined in these terms. But just as intimacy can become an addiction when sought for the sake of its own experiential "high," self-fulfillment can become cannibalistic when we feed on our own human nature. This is what happens when the longing for self-fulfillment succumbs to a craving for indulging the self. As Paul warned in his letter to the Christians in Rome, when we turn away from our spiritual origin and destiny in God and become obsessed with our created human nature, we become "foolish, faithless, heartless, ruthless" (Romans 1:31). This kind of self-indulgence leads to the dehumanization of others and the devaluation of our own spiritual existence.

If it goes in a positive direction, self-fulfillment moves toward the spirit of the other with openness, trust and a commitment to uphold the other's humanity and spiritual life. When we find the spirit of another person matching and meeting our own spirit, we have discovered the fulfillment that goes beyond intimacy. This we call friendship.

From Intimacy to Friendship

The category of human relationship we term friendship almost defies definition and explanation. Dietrich Bonhoeffer, who found himself isolated from family and friends while shut up in a prison cell for two years before finally being executed by Hitler in early April 1945, discussed the nature of friendship often through his letters to Eberhard Bethge, his friend and former student. In a letter dated January 23, 1944, Bonhoeffer wrote to Bethge, "In contrast to marriage and kinship, [friendship] has no generally recognized rights, and therefore depends entirely on its own inherent quality. It is by no means easy to classify friendship sociologically."

Exploring the place of friendship within the other areas (mandates) of life—marriage, work and state—Bonhoeffer finally concluded that friendship belongs to the sphere of freedom and

must be confidently defended against all the disapproving frowns

of "ethical" existences. . . . I believe that within the sphere of this
freedom friendship is by far the rarest and most priceless treasure,
for where else does it survive in this world of ours, dominated as it
is by the *three other* mandates? It cannot be compared with the
treasures of the mandates, for in relation to them it is *sui generis;*
it belongs to them as the cornflower belongs to the cornfield.

Grasping for a metaphor that would capture both the idiosyncratic
nature of friendship and its commonplace beauty, he later wrote a
poem in which he spoke of the cornflower (in the United States called
"sunflower") growing in the cornfield as a symbol of a friend.

Not from the heavy soil,
where blood and sex and oath
rule in their hallowed might,
where earth itself,
guarding the primal consecrated order,
avenges wantonness and madness—
not from the heavy soil of earth,
but from the spirit's choice and free desire,
needing no oath or legal bond,
is friend bestowed on friend.
Beside the cornfield that sustains us,
tilled and cared for reverently by men
sweating as they labour at their task,
and, if need be, giving their life's blood—
beside the field that gives their daily bread
men also let the lovely cornflower thrive.
No one has planted it, no one watered it;
it grows, defenceless and in freedom,
and in glad confidence of life untroubled
under the open sky.
Beside the staff of life,
taken and fashioned from the heavy earth,

beside our marriage, work, and war,
the freeman, too, will live and grow towards the sun. . . .

Finest and rarest blossom,
at a happy moment springing
from the freedom of a lightsome, daring, trusting spirit,
is a friend to a friend.

Having watched the wild sunflower grow promiscuously amid carefully cultivated rows of planted corn, I appreciate the metaphor. Along
with herding the cows so as to keep them out of the cornfield, one of
my tasks was to pull the sunflowers that seemed to crop up each year
in every field. Perhaps this is what Bonhoeffer meant by the "ethical
disapproval" of friendship when it appears amidst the well-ordered
and structured relationships of life.

Marriage, work and the state are like the cornfield—well planned,
carefully cultivated and arranged according to prescribed patterns and
roles. The sunflower is a weed and must be rooted out in order that it
not rob water and nutrients from the rows of corn. We can plant a field
of corn, straight rows and all, in somewhat the same way that we can
construct a marriage or contract a worker. But we can't create and
cultivate a friend in the same predicable way.

How do friendships grow then, if we can't arrange them in the same
way that we lay out a field of corn and cultivate it in hopes of securing
a harvest? Like the sunflower growing in the cornfield, friendship
arises and flourishes through the interaction of three things: seed, soil
and sunshine.

The Seed of Friendship

During my boyhood, the sunflower's spontaneous emergence in a
well-prepared field in which only corn was planted was a mystery to
farmers. We well knew that sunflowers grew from seeds, but we
couldn't explain how the seeds continued to propagate and emerge

year after year. Defensive action took the form of rooting out the plant before it had a chance to form seeds; thus we hoped to end this generational proliferation. Obviously, our attempt wasn't always successful.

Without pressing the metaphor too far, I believe the seed of friendship is also a wild seed. Because friendship is a relationship of the spirit, it blows where it chooses, to use the language of Jesus concerning the Spirit of God. "The wind blows where it chooses, and you hear the sound of it, but you do not know where it comes from or where it goes. So it is with everyone who is born of the Spirit" (John 3:8). The seed of friendship is sown by the spirit when our lives are open to the spirit of another.

Most relationships have visible structures or roles by which they may be seen. Marriage is a social institution with cultural and legal status in a community. The roles and relationships of family life are relatively fixed and often imposed by others. Friendship, however, becomes visible only when there is an encounter, either by personal presence or through some form of communication. Like the glory of God, which is the expression of God by which he becomes visible, friendship is the "glory" of spiritual communion between persons.

In his prayer, Jesus said to the Father, "I glorified you on earth by finishing the work that you gave me to do. So now, Father, glorify me in your own presence with the glory that I had in your presence before the world existed" (John 17:4-5). Jesus did not glorify himself, but revealed the glory of the Father in all that he said and did. The relationship of Jesus to the Father, however, was invisible to the world. And Jesus was becoming less and less visible as the expression of God's love and power as he was moving toward the cross. In his prayer Jesus asked that he be "glorified"—that is, that he might become visible as the Son of the Father. This prayer was answered in the resurrection, when Jesus was glorified in the midst of his disciples as the "Lord of glory."

The sunflower is the "glory" of the sun, making visible the invisible light that gives it life. So friendship makes visible what no other human relationship can, the glory of the spirit in its freedom of response. For this reason friendship is the substance of love and the source of renewal for all other relationships. Friendship is "born of the spirit" in somewhat the same sense as our new life in Jesus Christ is "born of the Spirit." The seed of the new life in Christ is not our spirit but the Spirit of Jesus Christ sown in our hearts. The seed of friendship is likewise the spirit of another sown in our hearts.

In the development of our self life from childhood to adulthood, we are prone to influences that teach us to order our lives strictly along the lines of approved ways of thinking and behaving, thus conforming ourselves to the spirit of this world. "Do not be conformed to this world," counsels Paul, "but be transformed by the renewing of your minds, so that you may discern what is the will of God" (Romans 12:2). There is a "spirit of the world" that seeks to conform our spirit to the regulations and rules that block our spiritual freedom. "If with Christ you died to the elemental spirits of the universe, why do you live as if you still belonged to the world? Why do you submit to regulations, 'Do not handle, Do not taste, Do not touch'? All these regulations refer to things that perish with use; they are simply human commands and teachings. . . . they are of no value in checking self-indulgence" (Colossians 2:20-23).

"Having started with the Spirit, are you now ending with the flesh?" Paul chides the Galatian Christians, who have turned back toward regulations and rules under the influence of religious legalists from Jerusalem. "Live by the Spirit, I say, and do not gratify the desires of the flesh. . . . If you sow to your own flesh, you will reap corruption from the flesh; but if you sow to the Spirit, you will reap eternal life from the Spirit" (Galatians 3:3; 5:16; 6:8). By "flesh" Paul does not mean the physical aspect of our lives, but the self as spirit turned back on its own human nature. The "works of the flesh," as Paul lists them, are disorders of the spiritual self, such as enmity, strife, jealousy, anger, quarrels, dissensions, factions and envy (Galatians 5:20).

We sow to the spirit when we become the soil in which the seed of the spirit can take root in our lives. The spirit holds the possibility of friendship as the seed carries the possibility of the flower. Openness to the Spirit of God means vulnerability toward other persons.

We run the risk of being hurt by false spirits in the world, which sow malicious seeds in the soil of the heart, according to the parable of Jesus concerning the enemy who came by night and sowed weeds among the wheat (Matthew 13:24-30). In the same way, becoming open to the spirit of friendship as a seed sown in the soil of our hearts is to risk betrayal and even misuse of our spiritual openness.

Having suffered at the core of the spirit in early years, many people form defenses against the spirits of others and cut themselves off from true friendship. In so doing they have cut themselves off from true fulfillment of the spirit as well.

We must be discerning about whose spirit we allow to deposit seed in the soil of our hearts. We gain this discernment through trial and error in a spiritually mature and friendly community. But each of us must gain this discernment and become open to the spirit of another in order to receive the gift of friendship. This wild seed of friendship is all around us, if we are but open to its emergence amid the carefully cultivated and ordered roles and rules of our lives. Perhaps we have been too anxious to weed our garden and so protect ourselves from the intrusion of the friendly seed of the sunflower.

The Soil of Friendship

Sunflowers do not grow in thin air. Neither do friends. In the parable of the soils Jesus spoke of seeds that fell on the hard pathway and were picked up by birds, of seeds that fell in the shallow soil and quickly perished, of seeds that fell in soil filled with weeds and were eventually choked out. Finally he spoke of the "good soil," where the seeds grew and produced a harvest "many fold" (Mark 4:1-8).

The soil of friendship in which the seed of friendship is sown must be prepared, receptive and richly supplied with the nutrients necessary for growth. It is an ironic fact of nature that the sunflower grows best in the richest soil. This means that when we prepare soil to raise a cultivated crop, we also are preparing the best soil for the wild seed. We cannot save our best soil for ourselves and expect the seed of friendship to thrive where we do not provide water and nourishment.

The soil that friendship needs is a well-prepared seedbed cultivated with care and watered with promises. The seed catalogs from which gardeners choose their orders in the wintertime don't carry pictures of seeds to be sown in the spring, but photos of fully grown vegetables and blooming flowers to pluck in the summer and fall. The promise is pictured by the fruit, not by the seed.

The secret of friendship is the making and keeping of promises. Promises are pictures of what can be realized through the sharing of spirit. What has contributed most to the instability, loneliness and lack of moral character in our society is not the loss of traditional roles and family structure but the loss of binding promises. "Binding promises," says Craig Dykstra, are "acts which overcome the slipperiness and ambiguity of human intentions and actions grounded in self-fulfill-ment." It is not the breaking of promises that destroys the bonds of friendship, but the inability to *make* promises. Promise making is a renewal of a commitment to grow friendship into a fruit of lasting happiness, shared with another human being.

The vows that I use in wedding services incorporate a promise of friendship as well as of love. When counseling couples planning marriage, I encourage them to consider the importance of being friends as well as lovers. Friendship, upheld by promise, as Dykstra has said, overcomes the slipperiness and ambiguity of human inten-tions and actions grounded in self-fulfillment. Love must go beyond self-fulfillment to friendship in order to avoid the pitfall of self-indul-gence. These are the words I ask the couple to speak in giving their vows one to another:

      _____, I receive you to be my wife/husband,
    and give myself to be your husband/wife,

from this day forward,
as long as I shall live;
I pledge my love to you,
I will cherish and honor you,
I promise to be open and honest to you,
to be your friend and companion in life,
to stand by you,
in happiness as well as in hardship;
I want always to be coming to meet you,
and to create a place for our love.

The Sunshine of Friendship

The sunflower is aptly named. It will grow as tall as necessary in order to stand above the other plants. In full blossom, the pod, measuring at least a dozen inches across, turns toward the sun in the morning and tracks the sun across the sky until evening. Rotating from east to west during the day, it positions itself during the night to face the first rays of dawning sunlight in the east.

Without sunshine no plants would ever grow. The sunflower seems especially aware of this and has adapted its life to stretch toward the sun and drink as much sunlight as possible. By contrast, the cornstalk, like the hand that plants and cultivates it, maintains rigidity and resoluteness, as if pretending it has no awareness of the sun at all. There is no trembling in the cornstalk to betray its dependence on the sun. There is no graceful turning of the head in acknowledgment of the light from which its own life thrives. Only if broken down by the force of the wind, or finally weakened by the brittleness of its maturity, is the defiant cornstalk broken.

But with friendship, as with the sunflower, the sun's grasp pulls life out of any rigidity or stubborn defiance. Friendship begins as a wild seed in the carefully arranged field of life's roles and regulations and, like the sunflower, follows the orbit of its empowering source through the trackless sky. If the sun should leave its customary pathway and suddenly emerge from a different direction, the sunflower would be there to greet its arrival. Friendship has no set coordinates and makes no demands on the love that sets it free. Its freedom is as fixed as the promise of the sun and as free as the open sky above. While marriage ages, friendship retains its rituals of renewal. The human spirit is never so contained that it does not respond to the sudden glimpse of another spirit turning toward it.

The sunshine of friendship is the life and light of the spirit, which flows from a well fed by a spring issuing from the very being of God. In his conversation with the Samaritan woman at the well, Jesus broke every conventional religious and cultural rule of his day (John 4). To talk with a Samaritan was to violate the rule of his religion; to be friendly toward a woman was to transgress the rule of his culture. But Jesus was a wild seed amid the carefully cultivated rows of his scrupulous contemporaries. He knew well what his detractors were saying about him: "Look, a glutton and a drunkard, a friend of tax collectors and sinners!" (Matthew 11:19).

While the conversation between Jesus and the woman started when he asked her for a drink of water from the well, he quickly turned it toward a more spiritual need. "If you knew the gift of God, and who it is that is saying to you, 'Give me a drink,' you would have asked him, and he would have given you living water."

Like a sunflower turning toward the sun, the woman responded, "Sir, give me this water, so that I may never be thirsty or have to keep coming here to draw water" (John 4:10, 15).

More than any other human relationship, friendship may come the closest to touching the image and likeness of God in human form. When Paul speaks of the relationship of Christ to the church, he appeals to the "one flesh" relationship of human sexuality as a paradigm (Ephesians 5:31-32). That may well be. But Paul, who gives no evidence of having had a wife, and Jesus, who never married, both see friendship as expressing the essence of spiritual communion. In that famous hymn of love, 1 Corinthians 13, Paul sings of a love that empowers friendship as surely as that of marriage. While marriage is a metaphor of Christ's relation to the church as his bride, friendship passes beyond the language of metaphor to speak of the essential bond of spirit to spirit.

In the same teaching in which Jesus uses the metaphor of the vine and branches as a form of "abiding" in his love, he speaks in no metaphor when he turns to his disciples and says, "No one has greater love than this, to lay down one's life for one's friends. . . . I do not call you servants any longer, because the servant does not know what the master is doing; but I have called you friends. . . . And I appointed you to go and bear fruit, fruit that will last" (John 15:13, 15-16).

In a poem prescient of our contemporary preoccupation with finding self-fulfillment at the cost of our satisfaction with life, T. S. Eliot in 1925 wrote of "the hollow men."

We are the hollow men
We are the stuffed men
Leaning together
Headpiece filled with straw. Alas!
Our dried voices, when
We whisper together
Are quiet and meaningless
As wind in dry grass
Or rats' feet over broken glass
In our dry cellar
Shape without form, shade without colour,
Paralysed force, gesture without motion;
Those who have crossed
With direct eyes, to death's other Kingdom
Remember us—if at all—not as lost
Violent souls, but only
As the hollow men
The stuffed men.

Deep within the pretense of our happiness as a self-fulfilled people is a desperate hollowness of spirit. We have little sense of partnership in the creative tasks of life; instead we seek moral vindication for our lives by joining fanatical protesters. We need a sign or a slogan to define our cause. Our political as well as our religious passions are weak until attached to the larger-than-life personalities we idolize or patronize.

We live and move on crowded streets and work alongside people whose faces and names we barely remember. We have no real sense of companionship because so few of us know where we are going. We shop at convenience malls and eat at fast-food outlets, having little opportunity to share bread with those whose lives are bound to the same destiny. Without a sense of destiny we have no clear sense of direction.

We make friends easily and dispose of them just as conveniently when we discover incompatible opinions and irreconcilable differences. The operative term for our culture is "disposable, biodegradable containers." Much of what we pour our lives into, including personal relationships, aptly fits this description.

The struggle for equality becomes a hollow victory when the battle is won but the soul is lost. The quest for intimacy leaves a hollow feeling when the moment is gone and the memory alone remains. The craze for self-fulfillment excavates a hollow core of hunger that remains unsatisfied when the last morsel is consumed.

The emptiness of spirit in the soul of our contemporary society is not a God-shaped vacuum only Jesus Christ can fill. Jesus is not one to be drawn into the vacuum of life after we have exhausted the inner life of spirit. "When you search for me, you will find me," said the Lord through the prophet Jeremiah, "if you seek me with all your heart" (Jeremiah 29:13). We need to find all of our heart before we begin looking for God as a solution to our unhappiness.

Beyond our right to find equality as created in the image of God lies our partnership in making life a blessing rather than a curse for many. Beyond our need for intimacy as a fulfillment of love's desire for love resides the balancing value of companionship with mutual faith in a shared destiny. Beyond our longing for self-fulfillment as a hunger for recognition and happiness in life rests the spiritual joy of friendship as the boundary of God's presence—"where two or three are gathered in my name, I am there among you" (Matthew 18:20). With all of our heart, we can be found among the "gathered," not the dispersed. "For where your treasure is, there your heart will be also" (Matthew 6:21).

The Spirit of God blows where it chooses. It is the "wild seed" that the wind blows across the landscape of our lives. *Lord, let the seed of your Spirit take root in my heart, let the sun of your love shine upon me. Be blessed as the flower of my love and praise turns toward you all the day long.*

Sources and Suggested Reading

Note: Sources are listed in the order of use, not alphabetical order.

Chapter 3: Someone Else Always Gets First Place

Miller, Arthur. *After the Fall* (1964). In *Arthur Miller's Collected Plays,* vol. 2. New York: Viking, 1981.

Golding, William. *The Lord of the Flies.* New York: Capricorn Books/G. P. Putnam's Sons, 1959.

Chapter 4: When I'm Hurt, No One Feels As Bad As I Do

Hart, Archibald. *Unlocking the Mystery of Your Emotions.* Dallas: Word, 1989.

Brunner, Emil. *Man in Revolt.* London: Lutterworth, 1939; reprint, Philadelphia: Westminster Press, 1979.

Macmurray, John. *Persons in Relation.* London: Faber and Faber, 1961.

Whiteley, Opal. *Opal: The Journal of an Understanding Heart.* Adapted by Jane Boulton. Palo Alto, Calif.: Tiogo, 1984.

Dillard, Annie. *Holy the Firm.* New York: Harper & Row, 1977.

Anderson, Ray S. *The Gospel According to Judas.* Colorado Springs: Helmers and Howard, 1991.

Fry, Christopher. *The Boy with a Cart.* New York: Oxford University Press, 1959.

Chapter 5: I Learned to Keep My Own Boundaries

Frost, Robert. "Mending Wall." In *North of Boston.* New York: Henry Holt, 1914.

Roszak, Theodore. *Person/Planet.* Garden City, N.Y.: Anchor/Doubleday, 1979.

Dillard, Annie. *An American Childhood.* New York: Harper & Row, 1987.

Guernsey, Lucy, and Dennis Guernsey. *Birthmarks.* Dallas: Word, 1991.

Chapter 6: I Learned to Keep My Own Balances

Thomas, Dylan. *The Poems of Dylan Thomas.* New York: New Directions, 1971.

Guernsey, Lucy, and Dennis Guernsey. *Real Life Marriage.* Waco, Tex.: Word, 1987.

Meissner, W. W. *Life and Faith.* Washington, D.C.: Georgetown University Press, 1987.

Vander Goot, Mary. *Healthy Emotions: Helping Children Grow.* Grand Rapids, Mich.: Baker Book House, 1987.

Wolfe, Thomas. *Look Homeward, Angel.* New York: Modern Library/Charles Scribner's Sons, 1929. (Quote is from the frontispiece.)

Heschel, Abraham J. *The Prophets,* vol. 2. New York: Harper & Row, 1962.

Brunner, Emil. *Man in Revolt.* London: Lutterworth, 1939; reprint Philadelphia: Westminster Press, 1979.

Lindbergh, Anne Morrow. "Even." In *The Unicorn and Other Poems.* New York: Pantheon, 1956.

Chapter 7: I Learned to Count My Own Blessings

Miller, Arthur. *After the Fall.* In *Arthur Miller's Collected Plays,* vol. 2. New York: Viking, 1981.

Frost, Robert. "The Road Not Taken." In *Robert Frost Poetry and Prose.* Edited by Connery Latham and Lawrance Thompson. New York: Holt, Rinehart and Winston, 1972.

Von Balthasar, Hans Urs. *A Theological Anthropology.* New York: Sheed and Ward, 1967.

Lane, Belden C. "The Rabbinical Stories: A Primer on Theological Method." *The Christian Century,* December 16, 1981.

Bonhoeffer, Dietrich. *Letters and Papers from Prison.* 2nd ed. New York: Macmillan, 1971.

Small, Gary, and John Trent. *The Blessing.* Nashville: Thomas Nelson, 1986.

Chapter 8: Beyond Equality to Partnership

Paton, Alan. *Cry, the Beloved Country.* New York: Charles Scribner's Sons, 1984.

Anderson, Ray S. "Toward a Post-Apartheid Theology in South Africa." *Journal of Theology for South Africa,* June 1988. (Includes a report on my visit to South Africa.)

Garland, Diana, and David Garland. *Beyond Companionship: Christians in Marriage.* Philadelphia: Westminster Press, 1986.

Hauerwas, Stanley. *A Community of Character: Toward a Constructive Social Ethic.* Notre Dame, Ind.: University of Notre Dame Press, 1981.

Chapter 9: Beyond Partnership to Intimacy

Bradshaw, John. *Homecoming: Reclaiming and Championing Your Inner Child.* New York: Bantam, 1990.

Gibran, Kahlil. *Sand and Foam.* New York: Alfred A. Knopf, 1954.

Bonhoeffer, Dietrich. *Letters and Papers from Prison.* 2nd ed. New York: Macmillan, 1971.

Gibran, Kahlil. *The Prophet.* New York: Alfred A. Knopf, 1962.

Anderson, Ray S. *Unspoken Wisdom: Truths My Father Taught Me.* Minneapolis: Augsburg/Fortress, 1995.

Chapter 10: Beyond Intimacy to Friendship

Bonhoeffer, Dietrich. *Letters and Papers from Prison.* 2nd ed. New York: Macmillan, 1972.

Dykstra, Craig. "Family Promises." In *Faith in Families.* Edited by Lindell Sawyers. Philadelphia: Geneva Press, 1986.

Eliot, T. S. *The Complete Poems and Plays, 1909-1950.* New York: Harcourt, Brace & World, 1962.